Sometimes a Wheel Falls Off

Sometimes a Wheel Falls Off

Essays from Public Radio

Connie Cronley

Hawk Publishing

Published in the United States by HAWK Publishing Group.

HAWK and colophon are trademarks belonging to the HAWK Publishing Group.

Printed in the United States of America.

Library of Congress Cataloging in Publication Data
Cronley, Connie
Sometimes a Wheel Falls Off/Connie Cronley–
HAWK Publishing ed.

p. cm.
ISBN 1-930709-13-7
1.Autobiography
2. Essays
3. Oklahoma
I. Title

[PS3563.I42145R4 2000]

813'.54 80-52413
CIP

HAWK Publishing web address: www.hawkpub.com

H987654321

for

Phoebe

and with gratitude to
Phillip and Marty

Most of these essays were originally broadcast as commentaries on KWGS, NPR 89.5. "*Burnout,*" "*Five Star Bookstores,*" "*Salute to Tomatoes,*" "*Tornadoes,*" "*The Lost Art of Walking*" were published in *Urban Tulsa Weekly;* "*Cat Lovers*" was published in the *Tulsa World*. These articles are reprinted here by permission.

Contents

SMARTYPANTS.COM: Everything I Know About Life

LANDSCAPE OF THE HEART

KITH AND KIN AND CATS

ENTERTAINING CULTURE

SMARTYPANTS.COM:

Everything I Know About Life

ALICE BUYS A CHAIR

I've just bought a new chair. Such a simple statement, such an ordeal to accomplish.

Buying a new chair is like the rest of life; it's always more complicated than you think it's going to be. It takes longer, costs more and doesn't turn out like you expected. I live in an older house, built in the 1920s. It's a small house. I call it a cottage, which sounds quaint and snugly, and I hope it is. When I was buying this house, the Realtor's son, a little boy of about nine, said to me, "When you came out the door, you looked just like the grandmother on *Bewitched.*" So that's the image we make together, the cottage and I.

Inside, it's full of quilts and whimsy. Cats drip from the furniture like Spanish moss. I have so many bits and pieces inherited from my family, my religion might be a form of ancestor worship. There's an ironing board from my grandmother, a lamp from my great-grandmother, and a clay pipe from my great-great-grandmother. I use them all, except the clay pipe.

I have an occasional piece of upscale furniture, which means from an antique shop, but most of the furniture is from the flea market or garage sales.

I once told somebody that all my furniture is from the flea market, and he stepped back from me as if I had just confided that I had leprosy. But come to think of it, when he started talking about his new home entertainment system with wall-sized TV screens, I took a step back from him, too. And kept going.

The point is that my house is old and small, my furniture is old and small, and when I went bravely into the contemporary world looking for a more comfortable chair, I forgot that scale.

I found a wonderful chair, very comfortable and on sale. It's a new chair but reminiscent of the art deco period and in apple green. It was so 1930s it made me think of Dorothy Parker. I could imagine myself sitting in that chair and saying arch and witty things.

It was a sleepy seven o'clock in the morning when I greeted the truck delivering my new chair. The two deliverymen opened the back of the truck and there, all alone in the cavernous truck, sat my chair.

"It's so big," I said.

"Everybody says that," they exclaimed together, delighted that I was so quick and bright.

Then I realized that the stores I shopped in were larger than my hometown. The showrooms could hold several football fields. On display were double-king beds and gargantuan sofa units that wrap around several walls. The oversized chairs are named for their size, chair-and-a-half. What size homes do these people live in? What size are these people? No wonder my little apple green, art deco chair looked demure beside all that — a peony at a convention of sumo wrestlers.

The deliverymen wrestled the chair inside and by 7:30 a.m., there we were — the little cottage, the tiny furniture, the curious cats, me and the big green chair. It dominated the living room. It dominated the house. I think it's the stud chair of the neighborhood.

I sat in the big green chair, but instead of Dorothy

Parker I felt like Alice in Wonderland saying, "Help, I'm shrinking."

After much lugging and pushing, the chair found its spot in the living room and there it sits reigning over the house. Very big, green and art deco. It has inspired me to make foods from vintage cookbooks, tomato aspic and Waldorf salad. The period is right, but I find I'm making them in very large portions.

And here's a concern. Any day now, the new desk I bought will be arriving. I distinctly remember it in the store. It was small, a small white desk. Is it possible for a big green chair to smirk?

HOT DOGS AND LIFE

One Fourth of July weekend, overcome by the American way, I went to the grocery store to buy a package of wieners for hot dogs.

I went up and down a long meat counter examining the extensive selection of wieners: all beef, all turkey, beef-turkey-pork, turkey-chicken, turkey-chicken-pork, fat free, low fat, reduced fat, regular size, bun size, plump.

I was awed by the number of varieties, but a young woman standing beside me was overwhelmed by the choices.

"Oh wow," she said, "I had no idea it was going to be such a big deal."

"My dear," I wanted to say, kindly, "you really do have no idea. This hot dog selection is the mere tip of the iceberg. This wiener counter is a metaphor of life. It's all going to be more than you counted on.

"Almost everything is harder than you thought it would be. I think Dorothy Parker said that. Or Ring Larder.

"Do you know who Dorothy Parker is? Or Ring Lardner? Or James Thurber? Have you read them? Do you read, my dear?"

And she would answer, in the vernacular of her age group, "You mean, like books?"

"Yes," I'd answer patiently, "like books. Because it's very important that you read, like books.

"I worry about that. I understand that young people are not buying books, and I strongly suspect that means they're not reading books. I hope you're not one of them.

"I hope you don't look at the big selection of books the same way you do hot dogs and despair. Just jump right in, anywhere. Reading is easier than choosing the right hot dog and better for your vocabulary, spelling, imagination, thought processes and health.

"The thing to do when you're faced with something overwhelming, like hot dogs, is to remember the motto: *Roll with the punches.* That means be flexible, be inventive. Don't take it too seriously.

"The thing is, in life we don't always know there are going to be punches, or where they will come from. Those are the ones that hurt the most; those are the ugly ones with names like Betrayal and Tragedy and Loss. They are different from the little, mean, sneaky ones. The little ones are easier to handle, but they all hurt.

"That's when it's good to have a little literature under your belt. And spirituality. And self-confidence and self-esteem and education and integrity. If people came with a list of ingredients like hot dogs, those would be the important ones listed first."

Wouldn't it be great if people did have labels in English as plain as "Caution" or "Hot!" or "Tends to Explode"? If people were labeled with warnings such as "Lies when under pressure," or "Disappears when times are tough," or "Competitive and uncommunicative," it would make selection of friends and companions much easier.

But people aren't as easy to read as, say, a book. So we all stumble on, trackers trying to find a path through the woods and looking for signs. And hot dogs.

COMRADE COMPUTER

The other day, I found myself doing something I swore I would never, ever do.

I was playing Solitaire on the computer. And as low as that was, it was a moment of triumph.

I was not surprised to read about the $1.5 million, two-year study that revealed that people who spend a few hours a week on the Internet are lonely and depressed. Being on-line, the study found, reduces the feeling of psychological well-being. I could have told them that, but let me start at the beginning.

I had a nine-year-old Epson computer and a very simple word-processing package called Professional Write. It was not much more than a fancy typewriter — no Internet, no e-mail — but just right for me.

I can't remember exactly what catapulted me into the chaos of progress — a new writing project and well-intentioned friends, I think — but suddenly I had a new computer lined up beside the old one. The plan was to make a measured transition from my old computer to the new one. My office looked like a computer museum. And that's when the bottom fell out.

The measured transition ran aground. For some reason, my old printer wasn't working at all. And the new computer with Microsoft Word was as alien to me as the time I took Russian classes and came face-to-face with the Cyrillic alphabet.

This whole new system might as well have been in Cyrillic; the mouse, the toolbars and F keys were that foreign to me. Learning typing and shorthand in high school was never this hard.

"Oh, it's not so hard," people told me, "it's not that much different from Word Perfect."

"But I can't do Word Perfect," I said and there would be a look of slack-jawed stupefaction.

"You can't do Word Perfect?" It was more than a question; it was recognizing incompetence and ignorance of universal magnitude.

By then I was defensive. "No, and I don't have a microwave."

So, I had no access to my old computer and all the work on it. And the new one was so foreign to me, I thought "cursor" meant me because of the things I was saying to the computer.

Why is it that misfortune heaps up like a snow bank? Something went wrong with my car. Now I couldn't work and I couldn't go anywhere. I tried to think of it with Zen wisdom — blessing the obstacles in our path for what they teach us and accepting our powerlessness. But mostly, I took long, solitary, weeping walks at twilight. If I'd had a shawl I would have looked like the tragic heroine in *The French Lieutenant's Woman*.

Then I pulled myself together and began taking computer classes. I took them all over town: at the public library, with a computer teaching specialist, at Tulsa Community College. And I began reading computer literature, compulsively. No novel held as much fascination for me as curling up with thick books about Windows or Word. It was as magical as reading *The Hobbit* trilogy, and an equally strange world of adventure and terror.

Slowly the fog lifted, but what I still couldn't understand was Folders. Documents and Folders and Files, oh my! These were the creatures that haunted me. I could make Tables and Drop Caps and Columns like a whiz kid, but Save In and Save As was as foreign to me as здравствуй (Hello.) In fact, I suspected that computers and Russian were rattling around together in my head in a box labeled New Information I tried to learn after the age of fifty.

I wrote for advice — actually I e-mailed for advice — a writer friend who has spent a couple of years wrestling with her new computer. She has been victorious and just finished a book on her computer.

"I can't understand Folders," I told her.

And she answered, "What's a Folder?" She's still so nervous about losing her work, she saves everything on disks.

Now, I don't want to jinx myself, but I think that after a month of classes and practice and weeping, I've about got it. What helped the most were the classes, especially the other women in the classes. I suspect computer use is a gender thing. Males like to e-mail bad jokes to one another, play games and daringly experiment their way through the Internet; women research trips to Italy or work to master word processing. For me, just fooling around with the computer would be like playing with the vacuum cleaner.

Although there was that one day I discovered how to play *Clair de Lune* and Solitaire on my computer. After that, I knew, mastering Folders would be easy as пирог (pie.)

AWARDS SHOWS

Yum, here come the Academy Awards. I love televised awards shows, which is a good thing because there are so many of them. There used to be just two, the Academy Awards and Miss America. That was a very long time ago, back in the black-and-white era.

Now there are so many awards shows, I have a chance every other month or so to see the *au courant* gowns and to cry with the humble victors. There was a bad patch when I didn't know anyone on the awards shows. I still don't know a lot of them — who are all of those television people giving one another awards?

Now, I'm pretty current with the movie people. I know Ben Affleck and his friend Damon . . . Runyon. But all those anorexic girls! Don't they have mothers? Is there no one to tell them, put something on before you go out in public; eat something because you look like you're sick; and brush your hair for heaven's sake. I don't understand those hairdos, all sticky and spiky. I had a yellow cat that looked like that after a bath.

Besides the clothes and the hair, what I like best are the acceptance speeches. I love those heartfelt, sincere speeches of gratitude. Nobody ever claimed that actors are philosophers. Or high school graduates. But at the next show, I'm going to keep track of how many speeches begin, "Wow."

Isn't it heartening to see what happy family lives they all have? And what solid marriages. Most of them thank their spouse — for supporting their art, for making life worth living, for bringing meaning to the universe. It's reassuring to see a profession so full of secure marriages. I'll bet if they weren't actors they'd all be veterinarians or missionaries or ecologists or some other profession devoted to just doing good. Instead of just looking good.

One of my favorite acceptance speeches was by a dancer receiving a Tony award for a Broadway musical. It was Natalia Makarova, who has a reputation for being no cream puff. There she was in a turban and Russian accent, icy glamorous. In her acceptance speech she said she wanted to thank her husband. He hadn't helped much, she said, but he hadn't gotten in the way, either.

I like the winners who break down before our eyes and make personal confessions of various kinds. The more maudlin the better. It reminds me that they are actors who are trained to read what other people have written, and left to their own devices, well, wow, anything can spill out.

I won an award recently for an article I wrote about cats. A national award. No money in it for me — isn't that always the way? — but $1,200 for my favorite charity and a handsome plaque. A publicist called from New York and asked if I'd go on the *Rosie O'Donnell Show* if they could arrange it.

"Sure," I said. Because that little phrase "if we can arrange it" is a gap wider than the Grand Canyon.

But say the most unlikely, unimaginable thing happens and there I am on the *Rosie O'Donnell Show* talking about my writing award and making a thank you speech.

I'll comb my hair, put on something sensible, eat

a balanced breakfast and then I'll thank the role model that made it possible — my cat, Phoebe. It's my cat who teaches me about good grooming, a good appetite and no regrets.

"Take every day as it comes, Rosie," I'll say. "Get some sunshine. Take a nap and moderate exercise. Play a little. Be a keen observer of your environment. Chase something once in a while. When you eat fish, lick your plate clean. And don't ever go to bed wondering if you could have done better. That's the secret of being a happy cat."

VOLUNTEERS-YIKES!

I've been thinking about the call from the Capitol for more volunteerism and what I think is — Yikes! If anyone took politics seriously, this would be scary.

Not that I'm denigrating volunteers. I've been a volunteer. I've worked with hundreds of volunteers. I've benefited personally from the work of volunteers. I realize that the infrastructure of our communities depends on volunteers in every area — social services, health, education, arts, culture, religion, security. Believe me, I know the value of volunteers.

However.

How-ever. There's a conjunction that hangs over your head like a guillotine. I have also known volunteers so diabolical they make Grendel in *Beowolf* look like Shirley Temple.

I don't mean the well-intentioned volunteer who is misinformed or untrained, the volunteer who cannot operate the cash register or the credit card machine, who doesn't know where anything is or how to find it or how to get there from here. Some very sweet volunteers at a museum couldn't tell me anything about the historic gardens, or how to get to them, although one thought she had seen them from a window, and another one gave me the home number of the volunteer in charge of volunteers and said if I called, maybe this volunteer could help me

I don't even mean the volunteers who are cranky, short-tempered or rude. I'm talking about the volunteers with their own agenda, volunteers who are mean-spirited, angry, rigid, self-serving, haughty and filled with hubris. And worst of all, self-righteous. They carry it like a big shield: "Don't even think about criticizing me because I'm giving my time."

But think about the things people give us that we don't want: colds, bad advice, wrong directions, rude gestures, narrow-minded opinions. Someone once gave me a punch in the nose that I really didn't want.

My favorite aunt loves to give me homemade cookies, but she's a terrible cook. They look good, but they're usually burned on the bottom. I once pointed this out to her, and she picked one up, turned it over, inspected it, replied, "Oh, hell" and kept packaging the cookies to take with me.

So maybe we need to think through this volunteer thing. Whatever we give — our time, our expertise, our money — are we giving it, bestowing it, freely as a gift? As a present wrapped with a bow and no strings attached?

Or do we expect something back, something like control, power, indebtedness. I classify this kind of volunteer work closer to a punch in the nose than to my aunt's cookies.

A TRAGEDY WITH HAIR

I've just come through a tragic episode with my hair. Although I'm not completely out of the woods, I am feeling a lot better.

This incident with my hair developed slowly. I didn't notice the warning signs. Then, one day, I realized how bad things were. I needed to go to Kansas City to meet some new clients and I kept postponing it. I could not meet people for the first time, especially for something important, looking like this.

Meanwhile, I wasn't get any work done because I kept drifting past a mirror to see if it was as bad as I thought. And it was.

I was also spending a lot of time and money on expensive professional care and, out of desperation, various home remedies. Many days, I abandoned all hope and just tied it back with a ribbon.

About this time I noticed I was wearing strange clothes. Either a dowdy Who Cares ensemble, or something ethnic and garish to draw attention away from my hair. That's when a warning bell went off. I thought about the questionnaires I'd seen about phobias, addiction and mental health. They usually included some form of the question: Is this interfering with your daily life and work?

One day I saw a revealing documentary on TV and I realized how low I had sunk. I called my sister in Tucson. Who better to turn to in a crisis than a sister?

"I know what's wrong with my hair," I said. "I saw a documentary about Albert Einstein and that's it. I look exactly like Albert Einstein. Except he had a big, bushy mustache and thought great thoughts, which was a compensation for that hair of his."

She thought a minute and then said, "You know, I think you could carry a big, bushy mustache."

I should have known better. Never turn to a sibling for compassion. Siblings can hold grudges for decades. They just wait to catch you in a weak moment. This was not about my hair. This was about time she was going to visit her son and wanted to stay in a motel or hotel, but the town was so small, there wasn't one.

"There is a bed and breakfast, though," her son told her.

"Great," she said. "That sounds good. Make me a reservation there."

"Yeah," he said slowly, "but there's something you ought to know. Until last month, it was a mortuary."

I found this very funny and always referred to it as the Saga of the Eternal Rest B&B. She never laughed with me. I should have known that she was waiting to strike back. So, forget sisters.

And forget men. You can't talk to men about hair. I once had a new, very chi-chi, short hairdo and a husband who looked at me and said, "You look exactly like Woody Woodpecker."

Most men have learned how to make superficially correct responses — "Your hair looks great"— but that's not the same as a gut understanding.

When it comes to gut understanding about hair, you need women friends. It was my women friends near and far who got me through this recent crisis.

"Something tragic has happened to my hair," I exclaimed and instantly we were talking the same language.

First, they sympathized. Then they told me about awful experiences of their own. Finally, they offered suggestions. "Have you tried cut? Color? Condition? Curl?"

"Yes," I'd say, "all of that. In various combinations."

"How awful," they said and I knew they suffered with me. They didn't talk in generalities; they offered specifics, recommending brand names and beauty operators.

Slowly, slowly things got better. Whenever I saw one of my women friends, no matter what else was going on, she took a moment to comment on my hair.

"It's looking better," she would say. "Every day, a little better."

When there were setbacks, they didn't lie to me.

"I know how you feel," they would sympathize. "I've been there myself. Many times."

With a lot of help and support, I progressed from the Albert Einstein look through a sort of George Washington-do to an early Sandra Dee, which was not good, but at least it was presentable. People no longer walked backwards to stare at me.

I am happy to report that eventually I made the trip to Kansas City, met my new clients and they didn't seem to notice my hair.

This is a story with a happy ending. I discovered what good friends I have. And because of this painful ordeal, I have become a more compassionate and caring person.

I can't wait until my sister calls me with her next crisis.

PASSING JUDGMENT

Let's carp and complain about degradations to the English language.

Me first.

You know how little things that other people hardly notice can irritate you mightily? For the last couple of years, I've been watching with growing distaste the use of a certain euphemism in our language. At first, the word crept in like a party crasher and hung around the outskirts of communications. Now it seems to have settled in permanently and is acceptable in daily usage. I'm talking about the verb "pass."

I have nothing at all against this ordinary word, as long as it remembers its place and is used properly. It's fine to say we passed another car on the highway, that we passed a course of study successfully, passed along a message to a friend or passed a basketball to a teammate. It's okay to watch the daylight hours pass into twilight, to watch a river pass by tranquilly, to have a deed pass legally from one party to another or to see that Congress has passed a bill. It can be pleasant to pass the time with a book. It's acceptable to pass in a game of cards. Noble to let an insult pass, arduous to pass a kidney stone and hard to pass up a bargain.

It's painful to be passed over for a promotion, or to pass out for any reason, and it's not very nice to pass for something you're not or, as I'm doing in this case, to pass judgment.

Far down the list of definitions — and that's where I think it ought to stay — is the use of the word "pass" as a euphemism for dying. To "pass over to the other side" was once a melancholy term bordering on spiritualism, and to "pass on" was a term within some religious circles. It was a short hop from that to saying "passed away," assuming, I assume, that this was a gentler way of referring to the departed.

I don't see it that way. In my church, I was instructed to say "death" and "dying" and "dead" since death is a natural part of life, no matter how we try to distance ourselves from it.

When I taught journalism writing, I told my students to use the verb "died" instead of a substitute. To report that someone died is the most direct and inoffensive way to give the information, and it honors the person by affording him or her the dignity of death. As a bad example, I had a newspaper story about a bar shooting in which the reporter wrote that the victim had been "plugged through the head." That term might be fine in a Mickey Spillane book, I said — and then I always had to explain who Mickey Spillane was—but it is not acceptable in the honorable estate of journalism.

There are satisfactory substitutes for the word die: succumb, depart, demise, decease, perish. And there are slangy euphemisms: cash in, croak, check out, snuffed, give up the ghost, bite the dust, kick the bucket, shuffle off this mortal coil. But, I preached to the fledgling journalists, these are not respectable terms for everyday conversation or news reporting.

Sadly, the world has not sat at my feet and heeded my words. So now we find ourselves in the distasteful situation of reading or hearing almost daily of someone's "passing." When my time comes, I hope it will not be said of me. Let the obituary writer pass up the opportunity of inflicting a final earthly jab.

I used to tell my students that I knew of only one exception to this rule of reporting death with journalistic solemnity and that was the story of Frazier the Lion. He was an old lion, the equivalent of a man in his seventies when he was installed as the only male in a pride of lions in the San Diego Zoo. And there, it was assumed, he would pass his remaining days quietly. But not Frazier. In that pride of nubile females, he behaved with the vigor and virility of a young male. He fathered scores of cubs and still he flourished. He became a media celebrity and year after year the world marveled at Frazier's expanding brood of progeny. But, all things die, even great lions, and one day Frazier died. A newspaper headline reported it this way: "Frazier the Lion Has Gone to That Great Cat House in the Sky."

EASY, EFFICIENT, EXALTED E-MAIL

One of the things I like best about my new computer is e-mail, even though some say this is a sacrilege.

"E-mail! And you a writer," my friend exclaimed. "E-mail goes against everything you stand for."

I don't agree. The way I see it, e-mail is another way to write.

What I'm trying to learn in life is to appreciate this and that, instead of this or that. For example, as much as I value a computer's research capabilities, I also revere old-fashioned library research — paging through the card catalog, ambling through the open shelves. A computer can be focused, but these other techniques suggest possibilities, connections, crossovers I hadn't considered. Often I stumble across valuable information while looking for something else, and not only in the library.

In one of the multitude of computer classes I've taken recently, a very young instructor was praising e-mail. "It's bringing back the art of letter writing," she said. Well, I wouldn't go that far. E-mail is nothing like letter writing. It's functional, it's fast, it's efficient, but it still involves the impersonal element of communicating with a machine. Like singing to the microwave.

E-mail has its own place in communication. It's not as intrusive as the telephone, for example. A phone is too clamoring and demanding. I like answering machines, but they can be frustrating. I finally get a return call I've waited for: "Hello, this is Vicki. You've been trying to contact me about an appointment. Well, you can reach me today only at (mumble mumble)." What? What did she say? What number?

The only thing worse is no answering machine. I was waiting to do an interview with a model in Italy who had to call me between fashion shows and could not leave a number for me to call her. So all one weekend I waited by the phone. I had forgotten the agony of waiting for the phone to ring.

I like faxes. They clatter noisily, but in *writing* and they wait patiently like paper soldiers standing at attention.

I like the way e-mail messages slide in silently as fish and lie there quietly. I like the speedy, telegraphic communication style. It's a shorthand way to touch base and to check in with friends, much like calling out greetings as we pass one another on the bicycle path. For business, e-mail is an unobtrusive way to confirm business meetings or give quick reports. A down side is that I've learned through e-mail how bad my spelling has become since I've leaned heavily on the computer's crutch of spell-check.

Checking my e-mail throughout the day has become one of my favorite things. It's a wonderful new way to avoid work. Playing Solitaire is a coarse and obvious type of avoidance and it makes me feel guilty.

Still, with very few exceptions, e-mail communications are not in the same galaxy as real, honest-to-god letters. I've talked about this to a librarian, an archivist and a literature professor — people I know will agree with me. Real letters tell us so much more than the words themselves. The way they're written — the speed, the mistakes, the size of the penmanship — tell tales about the passion behind the letter. Sometimes there are small, cautious words and tiny letters written timidly on the page. Other times the words are sprawling, expansive, obviously written in hot emotion. Perhaps they were written in such anger that the pen almost tore the page. There may be a postscript scrawled at the end or afterthoughts written in the margin. What are those stains — tears? coffee? Has the cat chewed one corner of the page? Remember writing love letters and spraying them with perfume? And the long, long letters from lonely friends?

With pen-on-paper letters, life spills through.

I like almost everything about real letters. I like to read collections of letters, especially letters of writers. What better way to get inside a life. I like to read about letters. Winston Churchill and his wife Clementine exchanged letters almost daily for the fifty-six years of their marriage. Writing letters, they said, was their private time together and the heart of their marriage.

I love to *get* letters; it makes me feel special. One of my favorite correspondents lives in upstate New York. We exchange e-mails, but we limit those to complaints and lamentations about computers. It's in our letters that we talk about what matters in our lives: our work, our gardens, our cats, our families, our trips and the books we're trying to read or write. A letter takes time — time to write, time to read. That's why it's like a present. It says, time is precious and you are worth time. Make a cup of tea, find a sunny chair and linger over a private communication. I even welcome those mass-produced Christmas letters in which an entire family seems to talk about itself in the third person. At least I know what's going on in their third-person lives.

E-mail, on the other hand, has a kind of a snap to it, and I find that I use that characteristic inadvertently. A couple of my friends' communication drifted into the shallows of someone else's life: a daughter's hairdo, a husband's hobby, a friend's accomplishment, the elaborate homes of acquaintances. E-mail was the perfect response.

"What about you?" I e-snapped. "What about your work, your volunteer project, your hobby, your hair?" Come to think of it, I haven't heard from these friends lately, but I'm sure I'll get a letter any day now.

And I mean a proper letter. John Donne never heard of e-mail, but he said this about communication between friends and lovers: "Letters mingle souls more than kisses."

THE LOST ART OF WALKING

I live in Midtown in Tulsa, where people walk a lot. We walk day or night, with a destination or for pleasure. Midtown is like a village that way.

There is no vicar or manor house in the area, but otherwise it is much like St. Mary Mead or Tilling. We would not be surprised to meet Jane Marple with a market basket over her arm or Lucia walking to tea. No wonder people walking in villages figure so prominently in English mysteries and gentle social dramas. People who walk see things. They talk among themselves. They think.

Walking is the transportation of choice for writers, poets and thinkers. William Wordsworth was a great walker, as were Walt Whitman, Jane Austen, Henry David Thoreau, Marcel Proust, Robert Louis Stevenson, Albert Einstein, Bertrand Russell, Aristotle, Hippocrates and Nietche.

"If I could not walk far and fast," Charles Dickens said, "I think I would explode and perish."

Dickens would be amazed to see what the modern age has done to walking. We have labeled it Self-improvement and have divided it into specialties: fitness walking, power walking, speed walking, race walking, Zen walking and more. We have subjected it to Meaning; we have given it Purpose. In other words, we have almost squeezed the joy out of it.

Thoreau walked half the daylight hours. His great interest, he explained, was "to observe what transpires, not in the street, but in the heart and mind of me!"

Today we could spend half the daylight hours

browsing among the books that tell us how to walk. These books explain walking from every imaginable aspect or goal: weight loss, fitness, stress or depression reduction, entertainment, vacation or adventure. (Adventure, one book says, can be walking from Nepal into Tibet or venturing into a new neighborhood. If you ask me, that is a walloping range.) The walking books tell us what to wear, what to sing and how to hold our arms when we walk.

Some of these walking books are as thorough as if they were written for people who have become earthlings overnight and have never put one foot ahead of the other. Maybe they're written for a tribe of people who grew up reading instruction manuals, who pound through life at a jog and parcel out their lives in dayplanners. For these people, walking will be a revelation. It's easy; you just climb off the wheels and actually touch the earth. You downshift and move at the pace of a heartbeat. You become part of the world around you.

I like to walk. Walking puts me in touch with the pulse of a place. Walking fast for twenty or thirty blocks in New York energizes me. Walking slowly though an Oriental garden in San Diego eases me into contemplation.

Midtown is safe enough and small enough that I can walk for relaxation or with a purpose: to the bank, the bookstore, the bakery, a restaurant, a convenience store or a drug store. I can saunter through the parks. I can walk to see the neighborhood storm damage, spring gardens or holiday decorations.

I do it all the time, early in the morning, at night and in the rain. I meet all sorts of other people walking: mothers with babies in strollers, students taking a break from the University of Tulsa, people with dogs on leashes or trying to teach a cat to walk on a leash, couples of all ages, friends deep in conversation.

I like to walk by myself, solitary and reflective. This confuses outsiders, people who don't live in Midtown. I walked over to meet friends for coffee at Borders Books. They drove in from outside the neighborhood.

"Doesn't Connie have a car?" he whispered.

"Of course she has a car," she answered.

"Then why is she walking?"

"Some people like to walk."

"They do?"

And think of all the jokes that begin, "A guy walked into a bar . . ."

Here's one of them. "He was treated for minor injuries."

SHOPPING AND – GULP! – CLERKS

Okay, let's see a show of hands. It's November, so how many of you are thinking about holiday shopping and groaning with dread?

Part of it is shopping, period. But another part — and this is the scary part for me — is clerks.

Clerks today are not like we used to be when we were clerks, implying, of course, that we were efficient, thoughtful and courteous. That is nostalgic nonsense, but at least we were taught to look at the customers. Even when I filled in at a cleaners one hung-over Saturday morning in college and put all the customers' clothes in one hamper with no names, I still looked at them, smiled pleasantly and said thank you. Of course I wasn't there when they came back trying to retrieve their clothes. I suspect there was little smiling on that day of reckoning.

How many stores do I go into today — health food stores, pet food stores, drug stores — places with rows of cash registers where the clerks all talk to one another over the customers' heads. We, the customers, shuffle through the lines as if in an old prison movie; lowly, ignored and anonymous. The clerks don't speak to us. What's even more degrading, I find myself automatically saying, "Thank you" to the clerk. Sometimes the clerk answers, "You're welcome." Sometimes not. This is backward and I swear I'm going to stop doing it.

Occasionally, young clerks are snarling and scornful as if I smell of old age and senility and they are the *Lord of the Flies* come to this country, all brutal animal instinct, mean adolescence and working in shops.

Before I started school, my parents taught me to say the alphabet, to count, and then some toughies: to tell time (this was before digital watches), to tie my shoes (none of us thought I would ever learn that one) and, maybe a year or two later — O triumphant day! — to make change.

This was my mother's idea. We sat down with a stack of coins. She sold me imaginary merchandise and I had to make change for a dollar, counting up. "Sixty-seven cents," she'd say. And it was a little puzzle for me to figure out —"sixty-eight, sixty-nine, seventy," I'd say, giving her three pennies. "And a nickel makes seventy-five cents, and a quarter makes a dollar!" I thought it was fun. My mother thought it was practical because if I could make change, I could get a job anywhere. That was a goal back then, to be able to get a job anywhere.

Of course I didn't have to get a job in the third grade, but even as a kid I had jobs: newspaper routes on my bicycle or selling Cloverine salve door to door. When I was in high school, I had a great job — working at the five and dime store as a window dresser. It was an exalted position, but I also worked other posts. I could cut window shades, mark merchandise in the stock room, roast nuts and pop corn at the candy counter and take inventory. Occasionally I was assigned the job of glory, the front cash register. I was a whiz at making change.

Today's clerks rarely have to make change. The cash register does the math for them. But what technology can't do for them is interact politely with the customer. Or teach them anything about the merchandise they're selling. Many times when eating at a restaurant I have asked the server about a dish and gotten a shrug and this answer: "To tell you the truth, I've never eaten here."

I don't know why. All other employees seem to eat at their desks or workstations. The other day I went into a shop, a laid-back boutique, and the clerk came forward eating a container of refried beans with onions. Now talk about a smell! She followed me through the shop, pointing out merchandise with the spoon as she ate the beans. It got to be too much for her when I tried to actually make a purchase. She had to set the food on the counter by the cash register, and we handed the money and merchandise back and forth over the plastic container of beans.

After the sale, I did it again. I said to her, "Thank you for your help," and she picked up her beans and I would swear she said, "Whatever." Surely not.

POLITICALLY CORRECT GRAMMAR

One of the hardest classes I ever took was Mrs. Simpson's sixth-grade English class. She taught it for decades, which meant that generations of students dreaded it for the first five years of school, then wore it as a badge of honor once they escaped to the seventh grade.

In Mrs. Simpson's English class, we conjugated verbs and diagramed sentences until our little fingers were numb. We memorized the parts of speech with the help of phrases which resembled something out of *Wheel of Fortune.*

"Preposition," Mrs. Simpson would say and we'd shout back, "Anywhere a squirrel can go." Which meant words such as: to, with and from.

But we by god came out of the sixth grade knowing grammar forever.

In graduate school I took a class in linguistics and semantics. It wasn't nearly as rigorous as Mrs. Simpson's class, but it taught me something important about language — that it changes. Words and their meanings are not carved in granite; they change slowly and subtly, like the seashore under the effect of waves.

If this weren't true, I wouldn't be reading *Hamlet* with the original text in one hand and a modern English translation in the other. That's right, an English translation for Shakespeare. My friends laugh, but how long has it been since we've used the word *swoopstake*? As in, "It's your revenge, that, swoopstake, you will draw both friend and foe."

All of which brings me to the poor, suffering misuse of pronouns today.

A pronoun is a useful substitute for a noun. The book *The Transitive Vampire* gives this example of how redundant language would be without pronouns:

> Columbine combed the snarls out of Columbine's hair and scrubbed Columbine's body with the loofa Columbine's paramour had given the paramour's true love.

As another example, if Bob Dole had learned to use first person pronouns, think how dull Bob Dole's campaign would have been to Bob Dole's detractors.

To me, the most egregious offenders of mangled grammar are television broadcast personnel, probably because I think they should be setting a good example and not an uneducated one. Their biggest problem seems to be compound pronouns in the objective case. Such as, "Give the bribe to Margaret and me." Or, "The werewolf stalked him and me." Television broadcasters usually say: "Give the bribe to Margaret and I," or "The werewolf stalked he and I."

Mrs. Simpson would sort them out in short order. "You wouldn't be tempted to say, 'Give the check to I,'" she'd tell them, "or 'Why don't you telephone I sometime.' Use *I* if it is the subject, use *me* if it is the object. The rule holds true if the pronoun object is singular or compound."

It is amazing how many people use the word I incorrectly and seem timid about saying the word me. I suppose they're afraid of appearing unlearned. Perhaps they were corrected too harshly as young children when they said, "Me fall down."

A much thornier problem is the lack in the English language of a third person, neutral pronoun. In the sixth grade, we didn't have any problem accepting Mrs. Simpson's explanation that the pronoun *he* can refer to a male or it can be neutral.

For example, "Anyone who wants to go on the picnic should write *his* phone number on the list." We knew that in this context, *his* meant male or female, anybody who wanted to go on the picnic.

Life is more complicated now. We are more gender conscious. So we might say, "Anyone who wants to go should write *their* phone number on the list." We become grammatically ignorant in an effort to be politically correct. Politically correct? Are you kidding? Nobody's been politically correct since Mamie Eisenhower wore hats and gloves in public.

It's a messy problem. We don't want to use the neutral pronoun *one* because it sounds affected. "Anybody who wants a free beer should raise one's hand."

We try using both pronouns together — *his/her* — but that's so clumsy it flashes like a neon sign. Uh oh, we think when we see *his/her*; got a radical feminist on our hands. Next thing we know, he/she will be raving about rewriting the Bible to make that language more gender sensitive.

One book I read tried handling this problem by alternating pronouns chapter by chapter, *he* in one chapter and *she* in the next. It had a swirling effect that left me dizzy and vaguely gender-confused.

In a ham-handed attempt to avoid offending females, feminists or the gender sensitive, we offend the educated — or should I say, the grammatically sensitive.

I don't have a solution. Maybe we should invent a

new gender-free pronoun, or, use the neutral *it* as in, "The dog wagged its tail," or "The writer scratched its head." Somehow, it will work itself out; language always does. Eventually, I suppose, the grammar will change and whatever the greater population speaks most frequently will become the acceptable usage.

To quote Shakespeare, "Zounds. I have never been so bethumped by words!"

DREAMING DREAMS

The other day, I had a phone call from my friends Dan and Molly. For the past couple of years they've been living on a boat outside New Palse, New York. It has been their dream to live on a boat, although not necessarily on a boat harbored in upstate New York.

When I first met them, Dan was the manager of a theatre in New York and the stress of his job was ruining his health. So they bought an inn in Connecticut where the workload of that quaint occupation — cleaning eight bathrooms a day and preparing breakfast for a house full of strangers — nearly pounded Molly into the ground. About that time they hatched this dream: they would buy a sailboat, learn to sail it, and sail away. Somewhere south, they thought, somewhere warmer than New York and Connecticut. So while they ran the inn, they shopped for just the right vessel, found it — a custom-built 40-foot sailboat — bought it, christened it the *Jolly Moon* and began looking for a school to teach them how to sail it. As they were getting their sea legs and building up their stash to live on, they sold the inn and Dan taught theatre courses in a college. Then, just before they hoisted anchor, he got cancer of the colon and had surgery and chemotherapy. He kept working at the college, largely because of the health insurance. Their beautiful dream had to be put on hold.

Even under the best of circumstances, dreams are fragile things. They fight so hard to stay alive like green plants growing through cracks in cement They need fierce protection and nurturing.

Sometimes dreams come into our lives fully formed, great and glorious in their vision, but let's not overlook their little cousins — a whole brood of them: daydreams, secret-longings and wishes. Wishes are the seeds of dreams.

I know a guy named Johnny whose friends call him "SomedayI'mgonna" because the leitmotif of Johnny's conversation is "Some day I'm gonna — buy a restaurant, move to Baja, get a Harley . . ." Some day he's gonna do lots of things, but he never quite makes a move toward that day. I'm sure people have laughed at me, too, but I'm grateful to those who encouraged me in my dreaming. It's not always easy to do.

I have friends who long and lament for solitude, for rest, for quiet. Yet any time off they fill with frenetic activity: a garage sale, a dinner party, a driving trip, fall house cleaning, anything but the stillness they want. They are always chasing busyness in the opposite direction of their wish.

What is our role as friends and supporters in this? Do we say, "Yes, I'd love to come to dinner or ride with you to see the leaves in Arkansas?" Or do we remind them of their little orphan wish for solitude left outside looking in the window?

Maybe we should all be mentors of dreams, offering gentle encouragement and nurturing our own tender wishes as they grow into sturdy dreams. Then, just maybe, more dreams will come true.

I have lots of wishes I'm watering like seedlings in a garden, and I have big dreams that, to my joy and amazement, have come true. Living on a boat has never been my dream, but I was cheerleader for Dan and Molly as they went from stressed New Yorkers to fledgling sailors. One summer I visited them on their boat in upstate New York and on a magical night we sailed up and down the Hudson River under a full moon.

So, I had a call from Dan and Molly the other day. The cancer is cured, the finances and insurance are in place, and in two weeks, they sail away. South, somewhere warm. I wish I were there to wave them off with champagne.

Eleanor Roosevelt said: "The future belongs to those who believe in the beauty of their dreams."

Boy voyage, Dreamers.

P.S. I had a postcard from Dan and Molly a month later. Postmarked, Beaufort, South Carolina. From there, the *Jolly Moon* makes its way to the Florida Keys and then to Belize. And from there . . .

VALENTINES, TAXES AND OTHER PHILANTHROPY

One miserable Valentine's Day, I found myself at my neighborhood grocery store buying cat food for the cats and a heart-shaped box of candy for myself, then having a blazing row with the store manager who didn't want to accept my check.

This was annoying because I seem to be at that store more than some of the employees. I didn't have my driver's license with me that day, and despite my regular attendance, the new manager didn't know me.

"Do you have any other photo ID with you?" he asked. "Like a passport?"

A passport?

"Darn, no," I said sourly. I had to bite my tongue to keep from saying, "and I usually carry it with me because you never know when the QE II is going to dock at the Port of Catoosa and I'll want to hop aboard."

To end that day in total agony, I went home and started working on my income tax.

Well, live and learn, you know what I'm saying?

This year I was looking forward to doing my taxes because I had some gauzy notion that it was an opportunity to tally up all my good deeds — my tax-deductible contributions. Then I would see in black and white what a fine, generous soul I am.

Shows you how wrong a person can be. I could have sworn my charitable donations were a lot more than that.

Beyond my own personal giving, I've done hard time

rattling the cup and begging for donations. For years I worked for non-profit organizations where part of my job was raising money. As a volunteer, I've been involved in fundraisers for charities. One year I was in charge of the annual fund drive for my church. Now I'm doing research about philanthropy for a book I'm writing on the subject.

I discovered that private philanthropic foundations are an American phenomenon. Until the Civil War, it was considered a duty by conscientious citizens to be personally involved in benevolent good works. Then people started giving money instead of time; it was easier and quicker. By the nineteenth century, the men who were making colossal fortunes from oil, steel and coal had invented private foundations to put a respectable face on their great fortunes. A new concept of American benevolence was born. When giving away money became a business, say critics of the system, the heart went out of charity.

My favorite definition of a private foundation was written by Dwight MacDonald in his history of the Ford Foundation: "A large body of money completely surrounded by people who want some."

The most famous of the titans-turned-philanthropists was John D. Rockefeller, described by the press of his time as "the supreme villain of the age" and "the most hated man in America." Currently, the Rockefeller Foundation gives away about $170 million a year, but it is no longer one of the largest foundations in the country. Newer foundations, such as the David and Lucile Packard or William H. and Melinda Gates, have endowments that are three to six times larger than the Rockefeller Foundation's $3 billion.

Although private foundations are more numerous and wealthier than ever before, and the nation is rolling in an age of prosperity, *The New York Times* reports that charitable giving is down. Most especially, we are donating less to social service organizations that support the homeless, the young and the hungry. Americans — corporations and individuals — do not seem amenable to sharing their wealth with the poor. It's easier, charities say, to raise money for churches, museums, universities, hospitals and the arts — organizations which cater to the middle class and wealthy.

Au contraire, says author William Upski Wimsatt who has coined the phrase "the cool rich kids movement." He maintains that these new millionaires have discovered philanthropy and embrace it as gleefully as they cradle cell phones. They're interested in "creative philanthropy," he says, which works for change, not charity, and is often "beneath the radar screen of the charitable world."

Okay.

Some of the great philanthropists were sad cases. Will Kellogg's psychiatrist said he was the loneliest man he ever knew. Then there was Andrew Carnegie, genuinely generous, who said it was a sin to die rich.

Closer to home, Tulsa was built by local philanthropists who have become legends — Thomas Gilcrease, James Chapman, Frank and Waite Phillips, Charles Page, Robert McFarlin and William Grove Skelly, to name a few. Because of his contributions to education, athletics and civic growth, Skelly's name is all around the town — Skelly Stadium, Skelly Junior High School, Skelly Drive Expressway and public radio station KWGS, whose call letters are his initials. Some of the Oklahoma oil philanthropists were colorful, high-stepping characters, but I am fond of the plain story of hard-working John Mabee, who amassed one of the largest fortunes in the state. He donated the men's residence hall, named for him, at the University of Tulsa and, directly facing it, another for women, named for his wife Lottie Jane.

Mabee was born in Missouri in 1879 and was so poor, he said, he didn't own a pair of shoes until he was ten. By then he had received all the formal education he was to have. He was a farmer, a ranch hand and a packinghouse worker. Then he began acquiring oil leases for the Carter Oil Company. In 1919, at the age of forty, he went into the drilling business for himself. His first two wells were gushers. By the time he moved to Tulsa in the mid-1920s, he was a rich oilman and he got richer. During World War II he bought more war bonds than anyone else in the state. About that time he began his philanthropic contributions, especially to universities and hospitals. He died in 1961 at the age of eighty-one.

He and Lottie Jane had no children. Maybe that's why he liked his money to go for buildings that bear his name. He had a compassion for the unfortunate, but no sympathy for those who would not help themselves. John Mabee was a self-made man who said the secret of his success was, "Work eighteen hours a day and don't forget that luck and pluck are partners."

KEEP YOUR EYES ON THE DOG

The first time I visited a pet supermarket, I couldn't believe either the size of the place or the menagerie. Most of the shoppers had dogs with them.

"What are all these dogs doing inside the store?" I asked a clerk.

"It's obedience class tonight," she said.

Ah, that explained it. So, on my second trip, I thought I knew the ropes.

"Obedience class tonight, huh?" I said to the clerk.

"No," she said, "that's on Mondays."

"Then what are these dogs doing in the store?"

"Shopping. Their owners bring them. You know, to shop. We think it's nice."

There were little slick dogs riding in grocery carts and big, drooling dogs walking beside the carts. Sometimes the people stopped to chat and admire one another's dogs. The dogs eyed one another warily or sniffed the humans. Occasionally, from somewhere in the store, I heard what sounded like dogs on the attack and people shouting. I became nervous and fretful and kept looking over my shoulder. I tried to avoid aisles with dogs in them. I grabbed my cat supplies and hurried out, trying not to show fear. I've heard that dogs can sense fearful shoppers.

If you are owned by cats, as I am, to enter a store full of dogs is unusual, even unsettling. It's not that cat people are less eccentric, but the cats are. My cats wouldn't consider being pushed around in a grocery cart. They prefer to stay home and have things catered in. I had a mostly Siamese cat named Abigail who was so shy, she hid under the bed for five years.

Besides shopping for cat food and kitty litter, I spend a lot of time standing in line at the post office, especially over the holidays. My initial response was to fume about it: there are never enough parking spaces, there's always a line of customers, there are always only two windows open. On and on I went to myself, honing my grievances to a sharp point. "Why can't the post office be more efficient?" I thought, frowning. "Why can't the service be quicker, like a fast food restaurant?"

A fast food restaurant? What was I thinking? Is that really the service I want to see emulated at the post office and everywhere else? If my whole world was like that, I'd be under the bed like Abigail.

When I calmed down and took the time to look at the post office, I saw that it has a quiet charm. Employees had put up holiday decorations, and clumsily, hand-lettered signs were tacked on a wall. One clerk wore a Santa's hat. The post office struck me as a village general store — chummy and personal. It didn't matter how many people were waiting in line, the postal clerk gave the customer he was with all the time necessary. Sometimes they compared cold remedies. When I wanted to buy 33-cent stamps, the clerk showed me the entire selection of stamps available and didn't hurry me to make a choice. She didn't seem to care how many people were waiting; my purchase was the most important transaction of the day. The clerks were patient, personable and sometimes funny. I recognized my neighborhood post office as one of the most pleasant places around.

One day as I was standing in line, I could see into the back room of the post office. It is an enormous room where mail is likely sorted and separated for delivery. Above the door was a big sign titled "Basic Rules to Follow." Obviously, these were rules for the mail carriers heading out into the neighborhoods. There were four of them:

Rule 1. Observe the area.

Rule 2. Keep your eyes on the dog.

Rule 3. Avoid signs of fear.

Rule 4. Stand your ground.

I like these basic rules. They could apply to any number of life's situations. I like them so much, I'm going to adopt them as my New Year's Resolution. Especially Rule 2: Keep your eyes on the dog.

Landscape of the Heart

ANTS

I've been very high-minded about gardening lately. But then, the summer is young and it's not yet a hundred degrees. Also, I just finished a class about earth-friendly gardening.

That was my frame of mind when the peonies bloomed. They weren't as cosmic as last year's blossoms, but glorious anyway. I love peonies. They remind me of paintings from the Metropolitan Museum and they make lush bouquets.

When I cut some and took them into the house, I found an ant. That was okay. Charming, even. I've read that ants help open the buds and are instrumental to the peony's blooming. Plus, I've taken a class about earth-friendly gardening.

"Uh oh," I said to the ant, "You belong outside." And I carried that one little ant through the house and across the yard to the peony bush and put it ever so carefully on a leaf.

In that moment, I was Mother Nature's Favorite Daughter. I thought: "I want a butterfly garden. I want to grow native plants. I want to garden organically. I love ants!"

I learned in my earth-friendly gardening class that the primary concern among horticulturists is water — the contamination of our water source. The No. 1 danger to water quality is not pesticides, as we might suppose, but nitrates from using too much fertilizer that washes away. The solution to this is to use slow-release nitrogen fertilizers.

Pesticides are the No. 2 threat to the water system because home gardeners use excessive amounts, which run off into storm drains and from there into streams and creeks. Also, we often dispose of pesticides improperly, such as pouring unused Diazinon down the drain. From there it gets into the sewer system.

When I heard this, I was awash with guilt. Have I ever done this? Am I out in the garden in my straw hat and hand trowel, waving at the neighbors and merrily polluting the planet?

It was all of this soul-searching and self-recrimination that led me to carry the ant out to the safety of the peony bush.

But then, a few days later, came the invasion of the ants. Suddenly, an army of ants was pouring into the kitchen. Every time I peeled a banana, opened a can of cat food, made a cup of tea, ants were everywhere.

I tried to keep them at bay organically with lemon juice, vinegar, ant traps and organic citrus cleaner. Child's play! Nothing stopped their relentless march to the kitchen cabinet. On they came — pom, pom, pom. There must be an anthill the size of Rhode Island under my house.

Some people call these sugar ants. I was calling them a lot of things, but not Sugar.

So I called in a hired gun, a friend with a bottle of insecticide called Dursban. One narrow line was supposed to do the trick. I checked with the master gardener at the Oklahoma State University Extension, then I attacked.

I put a little Dursban on a cotton swab and drew a line across the kitchen threshold. One thin line. Then, in my best *film noir* voice, I said, "Cross that line and you're a dead ant."

It worked. No ants in the house since then. I think I've got the message from the gardening class about being environmentally responsible: Use a pesticide only as a last resort. Use it sparingly.

And this is my contribution — speak in a firm voice, as if you mean it.

Think: "I'm Ida Lupino in the garden."

LILAC

Whenever I hear John Lennon sing "Woman," it summons up a memory of such clarity, I might be looking through a window.

"Woman, I can hardly explain ..." I hear the lyrics about not meaning to cause heartache and pain and I *see* the memory. It's a velvet summer's night, I'm in a honky tonk dancing with a guy I'm crazy about and that song is playing. The only trouble with this memory is that it never happened. At least not to me. Parts of it, maybe, but definitely not the dancing part. That's how I know it's not a memory, it's a fantasy.

Why is it that guys don't dance? In my real memories, the guys who are dancing are not dancing with me. In high school, I went to Teen Town every Friday night for what seemed like decades and in all that time only one guy asked me to dance. One time, one dance. That's because I grew up looking like Wally Cox in little pink glasses. I'd have given all the A's and honor rolls I could get my hands on, mine and everybody else's, to be asked to dance.

So because that John Lennon memory is so vivid, and so wrong, I didn't trust myself when I began remembering lilac. I was at a luncheon. It was early spring and the lilac outside the window was just opening into bloom with a scent that seemed to color the air.

"Every time I smell lilac," I said to the woman next to me, "it transports me back to my first years in college. My first apartment. Sheer white curtains in great puffs at the open windows. And everywhere, the perfume of lilac." Lilac makes you talk like that.

The woman had been sitting quietly, preoccupied. She looked at me as if I'd just read her diary. "Me, too," she said. "It's the lilac. It reminds me of college."

"And full gingham skirts," I said.

"And picnics by the lake," she said.

The memories tumbled out of us as fast as marbles rolling down a staircase.

"What are you two talking about?" someone called down the table. "What's so exciting?"

"Lilac," we said together.

A sigh went around the table. "Oh. Lilac."

"My grandmother's house," someone said.

"My first boyfriend," someone else said.

"'When lilacs last in the dooryard bloom'd,'" someone quoted. "Remember Walt Whitman?"

"And Edna St. Vincent Millay? And Carl Sandburg?"

"And Rod McKuen."

And we all said in unison, "Rod McKuen. Ahh."

Lilac does that to you. It gets you thinking about old beaus and romance and reading poetry.

Here's a little history of lilac. It came from Turkey into Western Europe in the sixteenth century. It was first planted in North America during the Colonial period. George Washington and Thomas Jefferson both planted lilac in their gardens. By the late 1800s when Walt Whitman wrote his poem marking Lincoln's death, the lilac was a quintessential American symbol.

And it smells like summer in heaven.

So many writers write about the powerful sense of smell: to arouse, to lull, to seduce, to tempt, to warn, to delight. And, for human animals at least, to summon musty memories with kindled emotion. Rudyard Kipling said that smells, more than sounds and sights, make heartstrings crack.

Here is one of my sharp focus memories. I had a boyfriend who had lost his sense of smell — he couldn't smell anything — and who gave me as a gift a bag of fertilizer for my garden, fertilizer so rank my eyes teared. His car smelled like it. He smelled like it. He didn't even know it. He was another one who didn't dance. I wonder whatever happened to him.

And I wonder what happened to Rod McKuen. Funny, I used to own a whole set of his books, but now I can't quote one line of Rod McKuen poetry. Some things just don't stick as tightly as the unforgettable smell of lilac.

CRAZY ABOUT SPRING

Here I am, being obsessive about spring again.

It's like a movie that I've seen over and over. First, it's winter and I'm sort of dozing through it, much like a hibernating bear curled up in a cave of fragrant pine boughs for the season. I vaguely remember Christmas, but everything after that is a blur.

Then one day — and this year that day was last Thursday — I find myself standing at the counter of a plant store and the clerk is saying to me, "That'll be $60."

"Sixty dollars," I repeat, as if waking from a dream. "Okay." And I stagger to the car, making trip after trip carrying snapdragons, impatiens, dianthus and anything else I can get my hands on.

Sixty dollars — and I know, compulsive gardener that I am, it's the *first* sixty dollars. I'll be back for more. And back.

I bought a mound of greenery and blossoms, enough to overplant the state of New Hampshire, but when I got it into the ground, it was a speck. As if my purse had spilled on the ground. Which is true in more ways than one.

And this is just annual bedding plants. It doesn't include the perennials and seeds I've already bought. And will continue to buy.

Layered on top of all of this like a gray, woolen pall is that admonition from the critics who surround me, saying, "You're not supposed to plant anything until April 15." Yea, even unto the plant store they follow me. Once I was buying a basket of primroses and a woman looked at me, raised one eyebrow, and said, "You're not setting those out now are you?"

"Who, me?" I said feebly. I felt like I was sixteen again, trying to cut study hall. So there's *more* guilt. Spending too much, too early.

As bad as this is, this compulsion with gardening, spring's obsession, doesn't end there. Oh no, there's spring cleaning, too.

I had a small, casual dinner party last week. I kept saying to myself, I'm going to keep it simple and easy and relaxed. I repeated that, like a mantra — simple and easy and relaxed. But by the day of the dinner, frenzy seized control and there I was, lugging the bed out into the middle of the room to vacuum under it thoroughly, taking everything out from under the sink to give another seldom-seen spot a good scrubbing. Waxing and shining and polishing, oh my.

There is a happy note to this story. Sometime just before the dinner guests arrived, I realized that I wasn't really doing it for them. I was doing it for me. The dinner party was a good excuse to fill the house with more flowers — pots of freesia, vases of flaming yellow and orange tulips, a gaudy van Gogh bouquet of red, blue and yellow suitable for the table, and in the bathroom, a tiny vase of elegant ranuncula from my garden. Flowers everywhere and they would be there long after the guests were gone. Flowers just for me.

A third obsession overcomes me every spring — the urge to quote Emily Dickinson. And no wonder. She calls this season "This Experiment in Green." She writes with happy madness about spring; she writes the way I feel.

“Modest let us walk among it
With our faces veiled —
As they say polite Archangels
Do in meeting God.”

JUNE

June is the month of brides, weddings and love. No wonder it's the month that rhymes with "looney tune."

I'm all for love. I'm all for weddings; I've had several myself.

But the more Junes I have behind me, the more I look at moonlight in other ways. I like the Chinese adage about love: One tear met another tear floating down the river. Said the first tear, "I'm the tear of a woman who lost her love." Said the second, "And I'm the tear of the woman who found him."

I've been those tears. I've been the river.

It's nice to see that there's more to love than romance. For example, June is the month of National Forgiveness Day, promoted by the Center of Awesome Love, which takes the edge off, but the purpose is still sound — to forgive wrongs. Even wrongs that the poet Shelley called "darker than death or night."

When we forgive, the Center of Awesome Love tells us, we give ourselves the gift of health and we set ourselves free from being controlled by another person.

June is also National Hug Holiday, sponsored by the Hugs for Health Foundation. It prescribes four hugs a day for survival, eight hugs for maintenance and twelve hugs for growth. That adds up to twenty-four hugs a day and, when multiplied, comes to 168 hugs a week. Which seems rambunctious and excessive, just like June itself.

How pleasant to see the whole gamut of love.

There's a French word for herbal tea, *tisane*. Balzak used it in a little verse: "Great love affairs start with champagne and end with *tisane*." In French, it sort of rhymes.

I think it sounds good in English, maybe better, because it has a sensible, clunky sound: "Great love affairs start with champagne and end with herb tea."

My favorite quote, at least my favorite this June, is from that frill of a movie *Enchanted April* about four English women who go to Italy on holiday. The character played by Joan Plowright is a dour matron with a walking stick who says, "I want to sit in the shade and remember better times — and better men."

MY LITTLE GARDEN OF SINS

One of the advantages of the numbingly hot days of summer is that everybody stops showing off their gardens. Finally, we can all sit down and rest. In late spring, there is a burst of social activity. My theory is that it is initiated by people who have great gardens. There is a scramble to get to the nursery, and then a frenzy to get outside where we weed, dig, plant, mulch and then host garden parties to show off our horticultural handiwork. This is a merry time, when folks in Shakespeare's day sang out, "Hey nonny nonny."

Next comes a longer, quieter period of maintenance and quiet replanting to hide our failures. Too soon, summer settles in to brood over us like a fat, yellow hen. These are the grim days of watering and whining about the heat and drought. Finally, about August, I say the hell with it and come inside. Sometimes I comfort myself with nursery catalogs, dreams of planting buckets of bulbs in crisp autumn air and then, in the spring, perfect gardens lush with tulips, daffodils, crocus and hyacinths.

I love to garden hop. I visited an extraordinary garden at a religious retreat outside of Boston. It was called the "Our Lady Garden," a tribute to the Virgin Mary. All the flowers were white, with one exception — a single red flower, as red as blood. The garden was designed to be the floral moral that none of us is without sin.

A memorable garden party closer to home was hosted by a gardener/gourmet cook. Lou made pizzas with dough seasoned with fresh herbs from her herb garden, and she cooked them in her outdoor bread oven that she had designed herself. We ate on the patio overlooking a blue garden, which she had created. All of the blossoms were blue. The garden was as blue as a pond, as blue as a Picasso painting before he cheered up. Nearby was a garden of yellow flowers for accent.

Another envious garden belongs to my friend Abby, who planted a long, arched cutting garden in the colors of the rainbow. From left to right, the blooms melted into rainbow hues: red, orange, green, blue, indigo and violet.

When I see such planning and control by amateur gardeners, I am speechless with awe and embarrassment. My own garden got the upper hand some time ago and shows no sign of relinquishing control. I came to gardening late and am self-taught, which means I operate largely in enthusiastic ignorance. I paid to have a professional garden design, but that was more to give me confidence than direction. Once I had it, I set out on my own in a headstrong, giddy way that seems to be my approach to all of life. The professional design is rolled up and stored in a closet along with various diplomas, certificates, awards and a menu from an Oklahoma City restaurant that named a hamburger in my honor.

There is a Zen philosophy that says how we do one thing is how we do all things. My garden bears that out. I've come to see my garden as a showcase of all my character flaws and shortcomings. It's my little garden of sins. Unlike other sins in life, these cannot be hidden away. These are in plain view for the world to see.

Lust, for example, exhibited as lack of self-control. That little red dogwood that looked so cute in the nursery? I had to have it for my own. I had to make it mine. I bought it on impulse, certain that it would grow the way I willed it. It chooses to grow into a squat, thick bush with miniscule blossoms.

Pride is another sin that dogs me in the garden, along with its toady companion

Foolishness. I so wanted an instant garden that I planted vinca in a garden bed as temporary filler; I put English ivy and bishop's coat near a walkway and honeysuckle along a deck railing. What was I thinking? No matter how much I prune and cut, these "vigorous growers" take over like the garden gangsters they are. Did I really think I could control them?

Greed is a sin that haunts me. I not only want all the pretty green things I see, I have a fatal tendency to see things as I want them to be instead of how they really are. Why did I think those little pear trees would stay small? What started out as a tidy row of green soldiers along the driveway, have overshadowed — and shadow is the right word — the roses on the fence.

Envy is why I have an unsightly bed choked with iris. I wanted stately spring flowers to rival my neighbor's. What I have is an undisciplined tangle leaning this way and that. The irises look as if they'd been on a drunken spree and staggered home at dawn.

Gluttony is what prompted me to plant a few crepe myrtles for summer color and bright yellow forsythia for spring. Now they have crowded out the climbing rose bush I loved.

Sloth prevails, which is why the little cottage garden

I aspired to is now a tangled mess. Everything has grown so much taller and bigger and thicker than I ever dreamed. And it all keeps growing. Nothing stays in place. The plants at the edge of the flowerbed turn into bullies. They stand taller than the ones behind them, like naughty children in a school picture. Some flowerbeds look like a monk's tonsure, bald in the center with tall plants on the edge. Many of my plants lean sharply to the sun as if they are making a getaway from the flowerbed.

This plant behavior leads to ugly displays of **Anger** from me, accompanied by language so acidic the hydrangeas pale to hear it.

Every day in the garden I learn a basic lesson of life — that careless actions have dire consequences. What's worse, the nature of sin is such that it engenders more of the same vile behavior. Luckily, help for even the most hardened garden sinner is readily available. The first step to salvation is confession. I called the OSU extension office to ask the master gardener, rather petulantly, why my flowering pear trees have not flowered the last couple of years. Because, I found out, they're not getting enough water or nutrition, and that is because I planted them in the wrong place.

"Oh," I wailed, "I feel awful. It's my fault. I did this to them. I put them there and I've neglected them. I feel so guilty."

And the gardening expert told me what to do to help them recover their health. "Don't be so hard on yourself," she said, "a garden is very forgiving."

A SALUTE TO TOMATOES

It's July and here they come again. Tomatoes.

We wait all year for garden-fresh tomatoes, and then we're knee-deep in them. First we can't get our fill of them, then we can't give them away.

Everybody has tomatoes and tomato advice. People I don't even know turn to me and say, "Whatever you do, don't put tomatoes in the refrigerator."

The Great Tomato Debate focuses on ripening techniques. Should we leave a tomato on the vine until it's as red as a crayon, or does that promote cracks and flaws? Is it better to pick a tomato at first blush and ripen it indoors? If so, where? A sunny windowsill? Wrapped in newspaper in a dark cellar? *Avant-garde* folk wisdom says the best way to ripen tomatoes is in a paper bag because temperature, not sunlight, is the key. Even better, put an apple in with them — something about chemical interaction.

One of my favorite gardening books flatly declares that it is not humanly possible to consume more than five tomatoes a day. Those of us who are trying to prove this wrong are scrambling for tomato recipes — tomato sauce, tomato pie, cool gazpacho soup, tangy bruschetta to spread on crusty Italian bread.

Ah, what a fascinating creature is the ubiquitous tomato.

Did you know there are more than 1,000 varieties of tomatoes, and that the largest tomato grown was seven pounds twelve ounces?

Tulsa botanist Dr. Paul Buck provided this tomato trivia:

◗ The tomato is a member of the nightshade family, a deadly plant family that kills half a million humans ever year. The nightshade family includes tomatoes, potatoes, eggplant, peppers, Jimson weed, belladonna, henbane and tobacco.

◗ In the early 1800s, everybody assumed tomatoes were poisonous. In 1820, Col. Robert Gibbon Johnson of New Jersey set out to demonstrate that tomatoes are safe to eat. In front of assembled townspeople, he ate an entire basket of juicy, red tomatoes. His doctor declared that it would kill him, but it didn't. Still, the rest of the nation clung to their skepticism. The populace began eating tomatoes, but never raw tomatoes. Just to be on the safe side, according to *The Godey's Lady's Book* of 1860, tomatoes should be stewed for at least three hours.

◗ In the late 1880s, the troublemaking tomato was involved in a legal case. Under the Tariff Act of 1883, fruits could be imported duty free, but vegetables were taxed. So in 1886, when John Nix brought a load of tomatoes to New York from the West Indies and was charged duty, he protested. Any botanist knows that a tomato is a fruit, he said. The tomato case went to the Supreme Court for a legal definition. Justice Gray handed down the decision in 1893: "Botanically speaking, tomatoes are the fruit of the vine, just as are cucumbers, squashes, beans and peas. But in the common language of the people, all these vegetables are usually served at dinner and not, like fruits, generally as a dessert." So, according to nature the tomato is a fruit, but according to the law, it is a vegetable.

◗ A gardening tip from *The Old Farmer's Almanac* advises talking to seedlings as they are planted. This builds strength in the young tomato plants and prepares them for life in a windy world. "Whistling is even better," the *Almanac* says.

For almost 200 years in this country, the tomato has been slandered, persecuted, taxed, sued and stewed for three hours. Still, it has triumphed. Now, gardening books proclaim the tomato to be the No. 1 vegetable (or fruit) in American gardens. I don't know if this is because of, or in spite of, human help.

TORNADOES

I did not go to see the movie *Twister*. I prefer movies where characters and stories are more important than special effects. Besides, I grew up in Tornado Alley and know more about tornadoes than I want to know.

When I was a girl, I spent as much of the spring and early summer months in tornado shelters as I did above ground. We did not have radar, Doppler and sophisticated advance warnings of approaching tornadoes in those days. What we had was my father and my uncles standing outside in the back yard watching the skies. They kept in touch somehow with the Highway Patrol and the Sheriff's Department, who had men stationed out in the country where they could see even more of the skies.

When this lookout network spread the alarm, we dived down into the tornado cellars and stayed there for hours. It seemed like all night. All the family came. And all of the neighbors. Strangers passing by jumped in. Nobody was ever turned away during a storm. We were packed like sardines in that cellar which was always dark, damp and smelled of mildew and fruit jars of canned green beans.

This was the ritual from April to June, part of growing up in small-town Oklahoma. Years later when I became a journalist, I wrote a long, nonfiction magazine article about the state's historic tornadoes: Woodward, 1937; Muskogee, Antlers, Oklahoma City, 1942; Pryor, 1945; Blackwell, 1955; Tulsa, 1974. This was before the worst of all, Oklahoma City, 1998.

At the time I wrote the article, 1977, Oklahoma had more tornadoes per square mile than any state in the union. Seventy-five percent of them hit in May, between the hours of three p.m. and midnight.

Tornadoes are considered the most powerful storms on earth. Their kinetic energy is estimated at ten million kilowatt-hours, the equivalent of every energy source in the United States working full throttle for five minutes.

In a bygone era, tornadoes were the subject of tall tales and folk humor. Whoppers told of tornadoes so powerful that they turned a cellar inside out, changed the day of the week, blew the mortgage off a farm, pulled post holes out of the ground, sucked water out of a well and even made the cows go dry. One of the tallest tales from the Great Plains is about a man sitting by his fireplace reading a newspaper when a tornado hit. He woke up twenty miles away wearing a woman's nightgown. Now *that's* a tornado.

I was young when the tornado hit Udall, Kansas, in 1955, but I knew about it. It was such a big story, the whole nation knew about it. It hit at night and wiped out the little town. A Pulitzer Prize-winning newspaper account of that storm opened this way:

"Dateline, Udall, Kansas — This quiet town died in its sleep last night."

I used that example when I taught college journalism classes. It is an example of the classic journalistic style — simple, direct, understated. It is harder to write that way than you might think. That's why it is classic.

There is a story about a cub reporter sent to Kentucky to cover a mine cave-in and trying to write with the impact of that Udall, Kansas, lead. The story he wired back to his paper began this way:

"God sat on a mountaintop today and surveyed the disaster that lay in his feet in the valley below."

His editor wired back:

"Forget mine cave-in. Get interview with God. Pictures if possible."

LISTEN UP, BUTTERFLIES

I was sitting on my deck the other evening trying to identify the butterflies floating through the garden. I had a copy of *Butterflies and Moths,* one of the illustrated Eyewitness Handbooks.

And I was trying not to think of the more idiotic business news I've been reading lately, stories about slash-and-burn downsizing, about executives dumbfounded to learn that putting people out of work is unpopular with the populace, about businesses lurching the opposite direction with upsizing and the new but absolutely sincere concern about employee well-being.

In those twilight hours, the butterfly guide and the business news blurred together. I imagined myself issuing a sharp business memo about the butterflies in the garden. The memo would read like this:

MEMO TO: Butterfly Management

Be advised that beginning immediately we will be running this backyard **like a business.** That means lean and mean. Cutting excess.

▸ Item One: Butterflies

These butterflies seem to be just floating around, flitting from flower to flower. I want to see a job description of said butterflies.

For improved efficiency, specific butterflies should be assigned to specific flowers, and they should move systematically from one flower to the nearest adjacent flower—none of this flitting all over the garden. This will maximize the butterflies' productivity. Repeat — no more flitting. The same goes for darting and swooping.

◗ **Item Two: Moths vs. Butterflies**

There are 170,000 species of Lepidoptera; about one-tenth are butterflies, which fly in the daytime and nine-tenths are moths, which mostly fly at night. Let's see a breakdown on our own butterfly/moth ratio.

(**Side note to Personnel:** Can we get moths cheaper? Is there a moth union rule against their working the day shift?)

◗ **Item Three: Identifying Types of Butterflies**

An identifying characteristic of butterflies is that their wings are held together over their back when they are resting.

Stop right there. Exactly how much resting is going on with these butterflies? Let's crack down on work time. Let these butterflies know in no uncertain terms that resting is to be limited to their lunch and break times only. No resting on the job.

And another thing. It's too hard to tell these butterflies apart. Let's get name badges for everybody and make it mandatory that said name badges are to be worn at all times the butterflies are in or near the garden.

◗ **Item Five: Migrating Butterflies**

These big, flashy brown butterflies I see might be Monarchs, which, I understand, migrate to Hawaii, Indonesia, Australasia and the Canary Islands. Check that out. I'm not authorizing travel expenses to Hawaii. Plus, do they have enough vacation time for that trip?

Some of them might be Painted Lady butterflies and these are the caterpillars that ate most of the hollyhock plants this summer. That stops immediately. Immediately.

Make sure the butterflies know that destruction of garden plants is strictly forbidden. Violation of this policy will be handled accordingly. The Painted Lady butterflies are welcome, but positively not in caterpillar form.

(**Note to Security:** Just in case these are Hackberry butterflies and not Painted Ladies, we might want to delete the reference to hollyhocks and make that generic — "destruction of all garden plants ..." etc.)

◗ Item Six: Trimming the Fat

We've simply got too many butterflies and some of them have to go. Work out a quota system so each butterfly will understand how many flowers it is expected to pollinate on a given day and ax the rest of them. Nothing personal, it's just business. There are plenty of other yards they can work in. Supply and demand, that's the name of the game, folks.

◗ Item Seven: Quality

We've got too many showy butterflies around here. We don't need flash. We just want to get the job done the cheapest way possible. It'll be far more cost effective to get plain brown butterflies for the back yard. Or moths.

◗ Item Eight: The Front Yard

Of course we need *some* showmanship for the front yard for the neighbors' benefit, so reassign some of the flashy, backyard butterflies to the street side. In fact, I think we can get even prettier butterflies than we have. Maybe a Golden Emperor from Australia, a nice Orange Moth from western Asia, a Blue Night Butterfly from the West Indies and a Large Oak Blue which is deep metallic blue and gathers in nutmeg and cinnamon trees in the Himalayas. Let's get some of these for the front yard. We can offset the cost by bringing in more moths for the backyard.

And another thing. I don't care if these are exotic

colors. We're not paying them more than the going rate for butterflies. In fact, we're going to pay them less because we have to cover the cost of their transportation. They'll probably be happy to get it just for the chance to get out of places like a nutmeg tree and come to our U.S. garden.

Remember, the standard of living is different over there. This is America, folks, not a cinnamon tree in the Himalayas. Butterflies all over the world would gladly come here for nothing.

I guess that's all for now.

Confidentially, I don't want this to go beyond the garden's upper management, but I don't see how we can justify the continued use of butterflies at all. I want to see a study of what it would cost to get plants that self-pollinate. That way we can cut out butterflies and moths entirely. Also, bees and a lot of birds. Cost-efficiency is the name of the game.

Starting right now, we're going to run this backyard garden like a Fortune 500 company. This time next year, folks, you won't even recognize this garden. Now, let's get back to work.

One last thing. Make sure morale is high. I want to see happy faces on those non-flittering butterflies and moths.

A WHOLE LOT OF STARLINGS

One evening I watched miles of black birds ribbon across the autumn sky, low enough that I could hear their chittering. There was an urgency about their flight, like a scene from J. R. R. Tolkein. Almost any spring day I can look out my window and see the green lawns dotted with black starlings. Sometimes just a few, other times enough to bake in a nursery rhyme pie. They are glossy birds with short tails and bright yellow beaks, strutting like rock stars and pecking in the grass. On one hand, it's a signature portrait of the seasons. On the other hand, all those starlings are a reminder of a literary project gone bad.

Starlings are not native to North America; they are birds of Eurasia and North Africa. About 1890, a well-intentioned Shakespeare aficionado wanted to introduce into Central Park all the birds mentioned in Shakespeare. That included starlings, so a few were brought, and the birds were so comfortable in their new American digs, they began to multiply. And multiply. By 1994, the population of starlings in the United States was 140 million.

I don't know which part of this story I like more — the folk legend of a handful of starlings imported because of Shakespeare's prose, or the census fact. I hesitate to question it because I know there are bird counters and systems for keeping statistics, but are we absolutely sure of the final tally of 140 million? I imagine someone in Oklahoma calling someone in Texas and saying, "Uh oh, here come a dozen your way. You haven't counted them already have you?"

But say greater minds than mine have solved this

problem and there *are* 140 million starlings — well, many more now since they multiply at such a clip. What do you call 140 million birds?

I checked one of my favorite reference books, *Brewer's Dictionary of Phrase and Fable*, to research the names of assemblages of birds and animals.

The correct phrase is a herd of antelopes, a sleuth of bears, a brace of bucks, a gang of elk, a troop of kangaroos, a pride of lions, a leap of leopards, a sounder of swine, a skulk of foxes, and a kindle of kittens.

But what about birds? Well, there is a cast of hawks, a sedge of herons, a murder of crows, a bevy of quail, a fall of woodcock, a watch of nightingales, a muster of peacocks, a nye of pheasants, a wing of plovers, a spring of teals, and a clamour of rooks. Nothing specific for starlings.

I guess we could borrow another of the technical terms for assemblages; perhaps a bunch, a cluster, a rope, a fleet, a clump, a pack, a company, a host, a team, a horde, a squadron, or a batch. None of those seems right, for so many of starlings. Or for a love of Shakespeare so profound it changed the balance of nature. Now that's something else for us to look up? What's the term for a literary love that intense? A passion, a devotion, an obsession, a dedication, an ardor, an enthusiasm . . .

OCTOBER

I had begun to wonder if the longest, hottest, most miserable summer in the galaxy would ever end.

It was Saturday morning, the first Saturday in October, and I was drinking coffee and reading the paper when I thought I heard a distinctive sound in the distance.

I hurried out the door, around the corner, up a couple of blocks, and sure enough, coming down the street was the Tulsa State Fair parade. A string of brightly uniformed high school bands from Oklahoma, Kansas and Missouri marched and strutted. They made up in rhythm whatever they lacked in recognizable melody.

A few floats with giant toys went by, a 4-H club, a beauty queen in an open car, and what appeared to be a girls' soccer team campaigning for a politician. The girls smiled and brandished signs that said, "Vote for our coach."

Horses with riders from the sheriff's department pranced down the street alongside red-hatted Shriners in mini-cars and zooming motorcycles.

Boys on rollerblades zig-zagged through the parade, clowns threw candy to the children and dogs dressed up in ruffs and funny hats trotted smartly.

The morning was slightly damp and cool — dare we think it was the edge of autumn? — and we lined the streets to see the parade. Grandparents with video cameras stood beside young couples entwined in each another's arms, but mostly the crowd was families with young children. A little red-haired girl, not more than five or six, was dressed in jeans and danced energetically to the bands.

Candy and Mardi Gras beads showered the crowd and children scrambled to retrieve the booty. An excited toddler beside me, inexperienced with parade protocol, kept the candy but threw back the flashy beads.

Another boy, maybe ten years old, watched this with cool amusement the way an older guy always watches an energetic young pup. You can tell already, I thought, he's going to grow up to be one of the coolest guys on campus. Maybe it was his laid-back style or the way he wore his baseball cap with just the right curve to the bill. He's going to be a heart breaker.

But the excited toddler, the dancing red-haired girl and I were anything but cool and detached. We clapped and cheered. So did the grandparents next to me, the ones with the movie camera.

My favorite parts were the bands with their uniforms in such bold colors — purple, scarlet or black with gold trim. The drummers were heroic. They must have carried those big, heavy drums for miles. They were mostly big boys and their cheeks were as red as apples from beating the drums.

Some bands had costumed mascots such as tigers or eagles. Many had baton twirlers who could fling batons, sometimes two at a time, high into the air and catch them. Squads of flag girls wore eye-popping costumes. Whatever the size of the girl or the fit and design of the costumes, on this one day they all knew they had been transformed into true beauties.

Those costumes reminded me that when I was a little girl, skinny and in pink- framed glasses, my Halloween dream was to have a Daisy Mae costume. I was only about nine or ten and didn't know the word voluptuous, but I knew that the only thing in the world that would make me not skinny and not bespectacled was a Daisy Mae costume.

As soon as the parade was over I rushed home, changed out of my end-of-the-summer pastel clothes and put on pants of hunter green and a brown cotton sweater — autumn colors. I went to the butcher shop and got thick, country pork ribs to be rolled in salt, pepper, thyme and sage and baked slowly in the oven. And to the grocery to get green Granny Smith apples for a deep-dish pie and sweet potatoes to be baked and mashed with butter. That evening, the house would smell of sage and cinnamon. And autumn.

"Tickle the earth with a hoe," Douglas Jerrold wrote in the nineteenth century, "and she laughs with a harvest." The State Fair parade reminded me that autumn is about harvest and abundance. So I shared my meal and made a supper basket for a friend: seasoned pork ribs, baked sweet potato and a miniature apple pie in a brown basket covered with a red and white checked cloth.

October is a month of contrasts — pumpkin pies, plum colored skies and gaudy sunsets — but also ragweed to endure, tons of leaves to rake and bag, the clock to be turned back and learning to live in the dark again like a mole.

There's all that Halloween candy to eat before the trick-or-treaters can get it, but it's also the month of World Food Day, a day the United Nations has set aside to make us mindful of hunger, malnutrition and poverty worldwide.

Shelley wrote that autumn is the season of "strange suffering when dirges sing in the wind." But Emily Dickinson, who could sing bleak dirges with the best of them, wasn't having it. She writes about "nature's ribbons" put on for the autumn party. One of her poems ends this way: "Grant me, O Lord, a sunny mind. Thy windy will to bear."

SACRED PLACES

I agree with Wordsworth — "the world is too much with us, getting and spending."

Sometimes I agree so strongly, I want to get away from everything. It was during one of those times that I spent a week outside Santa Fe in a monastery run by — I'm not making this up—a community of Benedictine charismatics.

I didn't know it was possible to stay in a monastery, but that merely illustrates how out of it I am, caught up in all that getting and spending. It has become trendy travel, I read in a guidebook "to escape the harried hustle of everyday life in a serene oasis of spiritual renewal in a retreat center guest house." That's what monasteries, abbeys, priories, convents and religious centers are called — retreat center guest houses. Most are as inexpensive as they are unique. My room with three hearty meals was $45 a day. The retreat centers, of course, would prefer that we guests not view them as a kind of funky adult hostel; that detracts from the spiritual element.

These beautiful, historic places are located all over the world. My guidebook listed Benedictine retreat centers in most states of the union and in faraway countries from Malta to Japan. The mood in these centers, I read, is quiet and tranquil. Meditation and solitude in beautiful surroundings offer a route to spiritual refreshment. A guest may take part in the liturgical life of the community, or not. A guest on a private retreat manages his or her own time; on a directed retreat, one meets regularly with a spiritual director. The abiding philosophy of the guest centers, I learned, is hospitality as defined in the Rule of St. Benedict and that is to welcome guests as if they were Christ.

The retreat center I visited was Our Lady of Guadalupe at Pecos, New Mexico. It was a dazzling October and I climbed in the Sangre de Cristo mountains, which is Spanish for Blood of Christ, and walked along the icy Pecos River, as black as tea. Sometimes I walked very fast, convinced that I had just discovered the paw prints of a large mountain lion. Sometimes I strolled down to the abbey duck pond and turned right, through the sweetgrass meadow. As I walked I ate tiny, delicious apples that fell from the trees planted by Trappist monks decades ago. A sudden breeze sprinkled me with golden leaves.

In the proper spirit of the place, I didn't use the monastery as a bed and breakfast. I went to the daily services. All of them: lauds at 6 a.m., Eucharist at 6:45, noon prayers, vespers at 5:00 p.m. and compline at 7:30. By eight o'clock, I was so spiritually renewed that I was ready to stagger up the hill to my hermitage and fall into my narrow little bed.

Lest you think it was a totally spiritual experience, while I was there I stole a dog and got lipstick on a monk's white habit, but those were innocent misadventures that could have happened to anyone.

Although it is almost too touristy to admit, during my stay I read *The Cloister Walk* by Kathleen Norris. This served as a wonderful manual, helping me understand and appreciate the Benedictine monastic community, the liturgy schedule and the daily reading of the psalms. The whole experience — the book and the retreat — changed the way I think about time, the psalms and community. It taught me not to see time as an enemy, always bearing down on me like a chase scene in a *Tom and Jerry* cartoon. It taught me that the psalms are poetry, history, prayer, praise and earthy emotion. Rolling on daily in a Benedictine community, the psalms become as routine as breathing or washing dishes. It taught me that a group of distinctive, even eccentric, people can live together harmoniously and that a community is like an extended family. St. Benedict knew something about families when he wrote his Rule in the sixth century. He admonished us to persevere, to be patient with one another, to forgive daily and to take a turn at kitchen duty.

Back in Oklahoma that same fall, I made several trips to Chouteau to research an article I was writing about Amish food. Under a gibbous moon one soft, autumn evening, I turned off the highways and away from the roar of eighteen-wheelers and followed country roads into Amish country. It was as if I had stepped into the Territorial past. Here is a rural community with no electricity or telephones. Horse-drawn buggies replace automobiles.

Away from city lights, the stars were strung so low in the inky sky that I ducked to avoid bumping my head as I walked toward Fannie and Mervin Yoder's sprawling white farmhouse. The night air was as crisp as an apple. The family dairy was part of the men's responsibility, but in this traditional lifestyle, the enormous kitchen was Mrs. Yoder's dominion.

The kitchen was warm and steamy; it smelled like freshly baked yeast rolls. There were about fifty of us gathered for a traditional Amish meal — the plain and simple country food my grandmother used to make. The meals are heavy, suitable for hard-working folk who are going to plow, harvest or dig the Erie Canal. This night we had ham, roast beef, homemade noodles, mashed potatoes, dressing, green beans, gravy, cole slaw, rolls, apple butter and two kinds of pie, lemon and coconut cream. Mrs. Yoder made everything from scratch. She had cooked all the food herself, using no electricity or appliances such as mixers, blenders or dishwashers. Three silent Amish girls with scrubbed, sun-shiny faces helped serve the meal.

Farming and dairies provide the primary revenue for the Amish, but to augment the family income, cottage industries are common: quilts, recipe books, buggy making, carpentry, fence building, storm windows, crafts and kitchen produce. Their crowning glory is the food that spills in cornucopia abundance out of the their shiny kitchens. Serving homestyle meals to groups of visitors is an acceptable way for Amish women to contribute to the family income.

The Amish do not advertise or seek publicity. In keeping with their religious and cultural traditions eschewing pride, which is considered a Biblical sin, photographs are expressly forbidden. "Graven images," one Amish woman explained succinctly. Instead, they rely on word-of-mouth and it works. Tour buses and groups from churches, schools and work-places in Arkansas, Oklahoma, Texas and elsewhere find their way along the gravel roads in Mayes County to the farm kitchens.

At the Pecos Monastery, the Benedictines wore traditional white robes and cowls, but underneath they had on practical clothes of jeans and sweaters. To generate revenue, they sell honey from the monastery bees and operate a brisk mail-order business of religious publications.

Fannie Yoder wore the traditional Amish clothes — a conservative, calf-length dress she had made herself, a white bib apron, a modest white bonnet, dark stockings and, a concession to twentieth century practicality and comfort, black Reeboks.

"Guests are curious about Amish ways and they ask lots of questions," she said. "Sometimes they ask if I make my own shoes, too." She laughed.

The Amish have a different way of life, Mrs. Yoder said, but it's not bucolic. "The Amish have daily problems too, but the Amish might not have as many harsh problems. Maybe I don't realize how harsh it is out there because I'm not out there."

Both the Benedictines and the Amish welcome guests to a traditional lifestyle where modern life merely peeps around the edges like lace on a petticoat.

This autumn in northeast Oklahoma, the leaves have been especially brilliant. Just a few weeks ago, the trees were green. Suddenly, the leaves flared like neon plumes — burgundy, fluorescent orange, lemon yellow, fiery red. I think the color was always there, under the green, waiting for the time we could see it. Just like the Benedictines and the Amish, such variety of cultures among us, waiting to be discovered.

NOVEMBER

It was a rare fine day in November — sky and leaves all shimmering colors—and I found my winter gardening clothes and went out into the yard in search of the herb garden to do some serious weeding. I hadn't been out in the garden since July.

When it was so hot for so long, I vowed that when cold weather came I wouldn't whine and complain. And I didn't — at first.

October came with its sunslant searchlight revealing all the dust and cobwebs and grimy windowpanes in the house. I was rendered speechless in the face of such obvious sloth. The lowest moment was discovering that the tile walls of the shower were dusty. How is that possible? A dusty shower? What a bad housekeeper I am! In that autumn light I felt like a suspect in an old B movie — a weasly character being interrogated by Sterling Hayden. "Honest, Detective, I didn't know I had to dust the shower stall!"

Then, a string of rainy weekends and November, gray, cool — such short days, such long nights. Luckily my office is splashed with sunshine or I'd never get any work done. But as soon as night falls — about, what? five o'clock? — I want to fall, too, into bed and luxuriate in these long, soft nights. It's still too early to be affected by the seasonal disorder of limited sunshine. I was just this optimistic early in the heat wave, when I said with madcap optimism, "Oh, how bad can it get?'

I'm sure that same folly will catch up with me in the dead of winter. But, for now, I layered quilts on the bed and, in honor of November and Armistice Day, began reading Barbara Tuckman's classic book about World War I, *The Guns of August.* No wonder it won the Pulitzer Prize. I read this book with slackjawed amazement, aware that my own knowledge of world history is on a level with Daisy Duck.

I read in *The New York Times* about the city of Rome's extensive preparation for its Jubilee year. In 1300 Pope Boniface VIII adapted the Jewish tradition of setting aside every fiftieth year for the glory of God. Ever since, the Roman Catholic Church has begun each century with a Holy Year and now Rome is primping with construction and renovation and the whole city is strung with scaffolding.

Coincidentally, I have a friend, Jan, who is planning her own fiftieth Jubilee year. She's been planning it for years and setting aside the money to spend an entire year doing all the things she has dreamed of doing — these months studying in Jerusalem, that month researching in Ireland, another block of time vacationing on Cape Cod. I, who cannot remember to take my grocery list with me to the store, am filled with wonder at this ability to plan so far ahead. Perhaps that's because I am so immersed in the lovely, lazy present.

I know winter is an ideal time to snuggle by the fire and read seed catalogs, planning next spring's garden. Maybe I'll do that. Later.

For now, I'm content to light scented candles, put on a CD of Puccini and burrow into *The Guns of August.* Waiting on the nightstand are new biographies of Lindbergh, Truman and Stephen Crane.

I'll plan later. For now, I'll indulge in November. And I'll remember this very appropriate poem by Thomas Hood from the 1800s:

> "No shade, no shine, no butterflies, no bees,
> No fruits, no flowers, no leaves, no birds — November."

PRAIRIE GIRL

It took me years to get comfortable with my native landscape. Through college I thought of Oklahoma as a place I would be from. Surely I would fit better in a more cosmopolitan place. Paris, maybe, or Greenwich Village. As a young adult, vacations were a kind of scouting expedition, staking out places I might move to — South Carolina or the west coast of Ireland.

I was teaching a writing class and using examples from Willa Cather when one of her descriptions of Nebraska gripped me. "The buffalo grass was like a great hide," she wrote, "and under it the earth was galloping, galloping, galloping ..."

That description was an epiphany for me. Suddenly, I saw a new beauty in the prairies and my homeland settled on me comfortably like a backpack. I knew who I was — I was a girl from the prairies. The prairie is home to me. I've felt that way ever since.

This summer, a college friend came for a visit. She's lived in Europe for thirty years, but she grew up in Kansas. For an outing, we drove to Pawhuska, had chicken fried steak at the Blue Stem Café and then on to the Tall Grass Prairies Nature Preserve. Although it's close and highly touted, I hadn't been there before. It was a shock. The sight of those rolling prairies and the slight scent of sweet grass had a visceral effect on both of us. For me, the strongest impact was at my chest, the place I had held a weak kitten I nursed back to health. I could feel the prairies in my throat, my skin, my lungs, but the strongest jolt was at my chest, my heart chakra. I looked at Michele and she was as weepy as I. This is what home looks like.

I have friends from Seattle and Halifax who burrow happily into a gray day, into mists and maritime scenes. That is the landscape of their heart. For me, it's gently rolling prairie as far as I can see. To some, a prairie is barren, but I see beautiful expansiveness of sunlight and shadow.

One of my favorite books is *The Great Plains* by Ian Frazier — a travelogue across that part of the United States once described on maps as "the Great American Desert." He tells tales of wonder about the place and its mythic people — Crazy Horse, George Custer, Billy the Kid, Sitting Bull, Woody Guthrie, Lawrence Welk.

One of the most powerful books about the plains is Gretl Ehrlich's *The Solace of Open Spaces*. Her memoir is set in Wyoming, where she went to work on a sheep ranch, running away from the death of her fiancè. "The arid country was a clean slate," she wrote. "Its absolute indifference steadied me." Her book is about grief and solace and about living again in a harsh and gorgeous landscape.

So with all of that literary and personal history, this summer I went to Spearfish, South Dakota. Big Sky country. The western part of South Dakota is the region of the Badlands and the Black Hills. They are called the Black Hills because distance gives the pine trees a dark hue. The Lakota Sioux consider the hills sacred. The story of how Spearfish got its descriptive name isn't very romantic; the Native Americans used to spear fish in the shallow streams.

Now the area is best known as the site of the movie *Dances with Wolves* with Kevin Costner. It is so well-hyped, I found some black-and-white postcards that say, "This site was not in the movie *Dances with Wolves.*" In nearby Deadwood, South Dakota, the casino The Midnight Star is owned by Costner and his brother Dan and the place is decorated with costumes, photographs and posters from Kevin Costner's movies. The items on the menu are named for his film characters.

I preferred Spearfish. The population density of South Dakota is nine persons per square mile, so I had lots of space when I went downtown. Main Street resembled a 1950s small town. The corner cafè served hot roast beef sandwiches open faced on white bread. Most of the customers were senior citizens, single working men or couples. The waitresses knew everyone but me by name. One woman was so attractive and theatrical she was obviously the local Something — writer, or artist or drama teacher. She had well coifed red hair, lovely makeup and was dressed in complementary colors of brown and rust. She reached across the table, seized the hand of the cafè proprietor and told a long, animated story that held them both in rapt attention.

Across the street was a coffee shop with a bookstore upstairs. The coffee shop attracted a younger set. A mother came in with a baby in a carrier and a three-year-old by her side. Students from the local college sat together looking bored. They were draped over the chairs and sofas as if they had been deflated. Three coeds were discussing boyfriends. "I like a guy who cries," one said, "but not like every day! He's like, If you leave me, I'll like drive my truck into a tree.'"

Other college students were so retro I thought I was in a time warp from the '70s — sandals, tie-died t-shirts and the girls with their brown hair parted in the middle and plaited in long braids.

One Sunday afternoon, I saw a cowboy on the corner looking up and down the street assessing his choices. He was dressed for going to town — black chaps, boots and a flamboyant turquoise silk scarf that fluttered in the wind. The wind threatened to destroy the effect of his hair, which he had combed carefully into a drakes tail and pompadour.

He crossed the road and looked at Main Street from that perspective. He looked at the café where some of us read the local papers and enjoyed the lunch buffet: sauerkraut and sausage, Swedish meatballs and gravy, hamburger patty and gravy, mashed potatoes and gravy, corn. For the fanatically health-minded there was a salad bar and pudding.

The café held no interest for the dapper cowboy. His choices were limited. The hardware store was open, so was the fudge shop where they sold miniature Christmas villages and collectibles. None of that was for him. He chose the coffee shop and that's where I last saw him, sitting alone drinking café latte among the retro hippies and the bored coeds, looking like what he was, a man from another world.

I left downtown Spearfish and drove up into the Black Hills. In the onyx night sky, the stars sifted down to rest in the treetops. The howls of coyotes circled my cabin where I curled up and read mystery novels, at peace, at rest and very content.

The Spanish writer Jose Ortega y Gassett said: "Tell me the landscape in which you live, and I will tell you who you are."

TULSA TIME AND SIGNS

After one year of celebrating, commemorating and general whoop de do, the City of Tulsa turned 100 years old.

Like any rollicking family party, we praised and damned the guest of honor with legends, myths and embarrassing stories from the past.

Here's my contribution:

An astrologist I know drew up the city's birth chart based on the date of the city's charter, January 18, 1898. Under the signs of the Zodiac, Tulsa is a Capricorn city.

What that means, the astrologist said, is that Tulsa is a city that is business oriented, solid and dependable. It thinks it is smarter than others, tends to cling to the past and doesn't like change. Sounds right so far.

Capricorns are diligent, determined, ambitious and charitable. I think of the brassy visionaries who built Tulsa, who built the first bridge across the Arkansas River, who acquired the railroads, highways (especially Highway 66), airport and the Spavinaw water system — all factors that enabled the city to grow.

But let us remember that the city's birth date is January, and that is the month named for the Roman god Janus, a god with two faces so he could look both backward and forward. I think looking backward is important in the celebration of history on the off chance that we might learn something to avoid in the future. Personally, I can think of a lot of episodes in my history that I don't want to repeat.

On the negative side, Capricorns can be overcritical,

narrow-minded and so interested in material things they are greedy. As author Danney Goble points out in his book of Tulsa's history, the city has flaws in its past, too, and not only the 1921 race riot. In the 1940s, there was inadequate spending for public health, and beginning in the 1960s, what Goble calls "an unfortunate and unintentional combination of factions" such as the expressway system, urban renewal and ineffective integration which contributed to a migration or, his term, "massive white flight" to southeast Tulsa where the mega shopping centers siphoned property tax revenue away from the Tulsa public school system.

We're still wrestling with the problems of balanced city growth, neighborhood development and public education.

Oh, it's all *so* Capricorn.

A Capricorn spends so much energy on career and prestige, there's a tendency to miss some of the human elements of life. But once Capricorns set their sights on a goal, astrologists say, the sky is the limit and they will reach the top of their professions — by hook or by crook.

There are other redeeming Capricorn virtues: responsibility, patience and — one of my favorites — a sense of humor.

As for me, I'm a double Pisces with a moon in Capricorn and a sister in Tucson.

AMISH FOOD – PLAIN, GOOD AND GLORIOUSLY BUTTERED

Research for a magazine article about Amish cooking took me to a pocket-sized Amish community in Mayes County in northeast Oklahoma. I was transported back to a simpler time in America, when community was prized and life was grounded in faith, family and a strong work ethic.

Farming and dairies provide the primary revenue for the Amish. Here are farms so neat and tidy, they look as if the fields have been swept with brooms and the barns polished. The Amish are a conservative, traditional people who drive horses and buggies. A glimpse inside the farmhouses reveals orderly rooms lit with the flicker of gaslight because the Amish do not use electricity. The rooms are hung with framed quotations from Scripture.

Mayes County, named for a Cherokee chief, was once the home of the Osage and then of the Cherokees. It is one of the state's top three dairy counties. Primary crops are wheat, corn, milo and hay. The first Amish settled here about 1900, when it was still Indian Territory. Nestled into 144 square miles, today the Amish population numbers about 500 in eighty families as closely connected and inter-related as a crocheted doily.

They are a fond and familiar sight around Inola, Masie and Chouteau. In the summer, shy, barefoot Amish boys wearing straw hats and britches with suspenders look like Huck Finn. Amish men are clean shaven until marriage, then their beards grow untrimmed. They wear no mustaches, stemming from a time in Europe when mustaches were associated with the military. Amish women keep their heads covered at all times and wear their hair parted in the middle and in a bun.

As fiercely as they cling to their traditional lifestyle, the Amish are not isolated from the modern world. Dairy machinery is often fueled by diesel and farmhouses by propane. The Amish do not own or drive cars or trucks, but for long trips they ride with "English" friends, their term for anyone who is not Amish, or they hire vans and drivers. Tractors are permitted because of the size of Oklahoma acreage. Sundays, however, they drive only the black buggies to their home-held church services.

The Amish are known as honest people, hard workers and good neighbors. "If there's a problem in the community," said Dawn Posey of the Chouteau Chamber of Commerce, "they turn out. They are there to help. It's like living in *Little House on the Prairie*." When a man's field caught on fire, she said, "here came all the Amish on their tractors with big water barrels. We were real glad to see them."

The early Amish settlers brought with them the tradition of German cooking, Americanized as the hearty, rural food of the Pennsylvania Dutch. As a cottage industry, some Amish farm wives serve home-based meals to groups. "It's the best food you'll ever taste in your life," a couple from Pryor told me. They were ten-year veterans of Amish tables. Amish food celebrates summer's bounty, autumn's harvest and the cook's skill. Many of the comfort food Americans love can be traced to German settlers:

sausages, frankfurters and hamburgers (named for German cities), cole slaw and pretzels. Amish and Mennonites brought the recipes with them from their native Germanic Europe, the Rhineland and Alsace when they immigrated to the Unites States. George Washington developed a love for the cuisine during his wartime months in Pennsylvania.

German-speaking farmers burned enormous quantities of energy working from dawn to dusk, and they needed calorie-rich starches and sugars to fortify themselves. Stick-to-your-ribs beans and ham hocks supposedly originated as "Amish preaching soup" to nourish the faithful during their long Sunday services. The tradition of plain and hearty food emerged as definitive Amish cooking. Today's Amish meals still include mashed potatoes and noodles and an assortment of desserts.

Other Amish women sell homemade produce from their kitchen — packages of thick noodles, the kind my grandmother used to roll out to dry on the dining room table, jars of pickled beets so purple they're almost black, apple butter the color of old port, jewel-tone jars of jams and jellies, green relishes, pickles and sorghum as dark as night. One woman near Inola specializes in *Cashew Crunch* candy made with only three ingredients — butter, sugar and nuts.

Late one September morning, I was in Mrs. Mervin (Fannie) Yoder's kitchen talking to her as she worked. By six a.m. she had done the family laundry on her wringer washing machine and hung it out to dry. She was cooking the supper she would serve to about fifty guests that evening, a church group from Muskogee and a doctor's office staff from Tahlequah, but just now she was taking a break from dinner preparations to make two desserts for a friend to take to a potluck supper.

"Fannie is wonderful," exclaimed a neighbor. "She will do anything for anybody."

Everybody calls her Fannie. She is so youthful and energetic as she runs up and down the basement kitchen stairs, it is hard to believe that she has four grown children. She is slim and radiant. Wearing a gray sweatshirt over her traditional Amish dress and with her hair in a bun at the nape of her neck, she looks like a ballerina in rehearsal clothes.

Eva Vaughn, an Inola resident and close friend for twenty years, talks about her mother's death in Missouri and how Fannie appeared at her side.

"I don't know how she found out, but she was the first one there and she stayed with me all that night." For the Amish, without telephones or automobiles, an emergency trip to Missouri is not effortless.

Mrs. Yoder is famous for her pie crusts and coconut pies. "Out of this world," one repeat diner exclaimed. The secret of being a good cook, Mrs. Yoder believes, is to love cooking. "And I love people," she said.

By mid-December, she will be serving noon and evening meals every day except Sunday. She cooks it all on two ordinary ranges and a convection oven. When she's not serving, she does not cook three hearty meals a day.

"To tell you the truth," she confided, "we get tired of these big, groaning meals. There are times I wish I could go to a chef's school and learn how to prepare gourmet food."

The modest Amish are publicity shy, but Mrs. Norman (Fanny) Miller, a woman as short and stout as a cookie jar, bordered on the uncooperative. Still, she is such a persuasive salesperson that I staggered out her back door carrying an armload of her noodles, bread, pickled beets and a Miller family recipe book. Her homemade dinner rolls were like handfuls of cumulus clouds.

I first met Mrs. Miller on a hot, August day as she and a slew of daughters, daughters-in-law and grandchildren were finishing their lunch in a great kitchen so shiny and clean the glare made me squint. The kitchen is the heart of the Amish home. Through the large plate glass kitchen window we could see foals gamboling in the corral. The family unit is revered by the Amish. One of her married daughters was moving to Missouri and the event was stressful for Mrs. Miller. "I just don't know how I'm going to stand it," she lamented.

Mrs. Miller's Cooking Tips:

- Make peanut brittle on a day when the sun is shining.
- Soak chicken in saltwater before frying it.

Most of the Amish women and children I saw that summer in their homes and gardens were barefoot, reminding me how this rural community preserves its close-to-the-earth lifestyle.

A few miles away, Chet and Beth's Amish Bakery is run by a young couple who raise hay and run cattle on their farm. Every morning, Monday through Saturday, they drive their red tractor to work at their bakery. Shelves are lined with cookies, nut breads, and gleaming jars of jams and preserves as brightly colored as Christmas tree lights. The main attraction, however, is the baked goods. Local residents prefer the fresh pies: apple, Dutch apple, pecan, custard, cherry, blackberry, peach, apricot, rhubarb, strawberry-rhubarb, blueberry, raspberry, coconut, lemon, banana, peanut butter and chocolate. Raisin pie was such a best seller, I had to special order one.

One Pennsylvania Dutch motto proclaims: *A meal without pie is no meal at all.* Some food historians believe that fruit pies, declared America's favorite dessert, were invented by the Pennsylvania Dutch and that Revolutionary War soldiers carried descriptions of the dessert home to other colonies. Raisin pie and shoofly pie were certainly Pennsylvania Dutch originals. The word "cookie" is from the Dutch work *koekje*, which means "little cake." Those early settlers had a great penchant for cinnamon, which contributed an entire genre to American cookery: cinnamon buns, cinnamon bread with raisins, ginger snap cookies and gingerbread.

An Amish farm bakery owned and operated by Anna Mae and Lloyd Ropp is open only Fridays and Saturdays and has become so successful it is eclipsing their in-home meal business. The bakery overlooks the Ropp's wheat field and, beyond that, busy State Highway 412. It is identified only by a small, hand lettered sign: *Bakery. Open.*

That simple sign and the bakery's reputation are enough to attract a steady stream of customers. Each weekend, 240 loaves of bread are baked and sold; white, honey oat, wheat and light wheat. Angel food cakes may be oneof the most popular items: the record sold is forty-five in two days. Angel food cakes are said to have evolved among the Pennsylvania Dutch farmers as a thrifty way to use the numerous egg whites left over from making noodles with egg yolks.

The Amish cooks I talked with, sitting around their kitchen tables, told me they rarely use recipes. They "picked up" cooking from their grandmothers, mothers and aunts, they say, and they rely on the "feel" of the pie dough. Mrs. Ropp, small and birdlike but with a fierce handshake, is not chatty with us English, but she is forthright.

"I don't know anything about Amish food," she replied to my journalistic questions. "To me, it's the only food I know." When pressed for recipes, Mrs. Ropp talks in commercial bakery volume: For eight angel food cakes, use sixteen cups of egg whites; to make thirty-two dozen noodles, use twenty-eight dozen egg yolks and four dozen whole eggs.

Mrs. Ropp's Cooking Tips:

- For flavorful noodles, cook them in chicken broth
- For crispy baked chicken, dip chicken in oleo and cracker crumbs before baking.

In the kitchen of the Ropp's farm bakery, a clutch of young Amish women wear white bonnets and colorful homemade dresses in rose, lavender, green and blue. They chatter among themselves in Pennsylvania Dutch as they work.

The aroma of cinnamon rolls trailing down the country road is intoxicating. Even the visual effect of the tiny bakery is overpowering. Shelves from floor to ceiling hold freshly baked cakes, cookies, fruit pies, cream pies, custard pies and crusty loaves of whole wheat bread just out of the oven. These wholesome baked goods, plain and simple, are so country they might be on their way to the State Fair. As if I weren't already teetering on the edge of gluttony, I discovered that the bakery also sells freshly churned butter. And brown eggs from a neighboring farm.

The butter is sold by the pound, a square block of butter so creamy rich in butterfat, it melts at the touch of a finger. Butter as yellow as corn, as yellow as daisy petals, as yellow as a summer's dress.

When I was a girl, I learned to drive by driving out to a farm where we bought our milk by the gallon jar. The cream rose on the milk halfway down the jar. My little sister, good and generous, always stirred the cream into the milk before pouring it. I was greedier, and whenever I could I'd scoop the thick cream off the milk and ladle it directly onto my cereal. My father did the same thing.

This block of yellow Amish butter was just a turn of the churn away from that thick cream of my memory. That's what I was thinking late one Sunday morning when I made a simple feast of a breakfast — thick slices of freshly baked bread toasted in the oven with slabs of butter and a couple of fried farm eggs with yolks as orange as a harvest moon. A squat jar of homemade strawberry jam was close by.

Then I realized that as I was eating this farm feast, I was reading an article about nutrition. Specifically about beans and legumes.

"Get hold of yourself," I thought. "Stop it this minute!" I had promised myself I would stop reading when I eat alone and focus on enjoying the meal. Be in the moment, as Zen teachers say. Which is a great idea if there is also scrumptious, golden butter in the moment. So I put aside the good article about legumes and thought, like Scarlet O'Hara, "I'll read about that tomorrow."

But, there was that fat brick of Amish butter on the counter. No, I decided, what I'll think about tomorrow is what to do with that sunny butter. Maybe I'll make lemon pound cake. And shortbread cookies. A nice sauce for vegetables, baked potatoes with melted butter dribbling over the edges, a rich and creamy sauce for fish. That's what I'll think about tomorrow.

As for today, I'll use some of that bright, pure butter and brown eggs and sorghum to make old-fashioned gingerbread to fill the house with the smell of country.

I'll do beans and legumes the day after tomorrow. With a pan of cornbread slathered with yellow butter. And for dessert ...

WINTER SOLSTICE

We're on the upswing now, but there was a bad patch around the time of the winter solstice when I couldn't stay awake. The days were getting shorter, grayer and colder, and I was always sleepy. I had trouble waking up in the morning, I couldn't stay awake all day and all I did was look forward to the time when I could trundle off to bed for the night.

"You can't go to bed at 6:30!" someone said.

"Why not?"I asked. "It's dark."

I was talking about this problem on the phone to a friend who is a poet.

"It's the winter solstice," she said, "and I have a theory about that." I grabbed a pencil to make a note of it.

"What I think," my poet friend said, "is that the winter solstice is like a drain. It's the end of the year going down the drain and we're going down with it."

I put my pencil down because I have to tell you, I expected more from a poet. I expected a better simile than "the winter solstice is like going down the drain."

The winter solstice, December 21 or 22, is the companion to the summer solstice of June 21. The name solstice comes from the Latin — *sol* or sun and *stitium*, to stand still. On these dates the sun reaches its extreme southern and northern points in its heavenly track and appears to stand still before it turns back on its apparent course.

Maybe I'm sleepy because the winter solstice is the shortest day of the year. The winter solstice, a.k.a. Midwinter or Yuletide, has been celebrated since ancient times, so perhaps it's the weight of history that is lulling me to sleep, much like climbing under a down-filled comforter.

The winter that closed in around my aboriginal ancestors in the northern latitudes was a scary time. The growing season was long over and game was scarce. What would happen to them, they wondered, if the sun disappeared forever and left them in permanent darkness and cold? No wonder they rejoiced at the winter solstice when the sun seemed to gather strength again.

In ancient Egypt, Osiris died and was entombed December 21; but at midnight the priests emerged crying, "The Virgin has brought forth. The light is waxing." Then they showed the image of a baby to the worshipers. By the third century, the Roman Empire had braided together a slew of pagan solstice celebrations and called the December 25 festival the Birthday of the Unconquered Sun.

Wherever it was observed, the winter solstice was associated with rebirth and introspection. It was a time to hold fast to faith, even in the dead of winter. The celebration was a time of music, bonfires and feasts honoring the sun. In distant ages, too, it was a time of family celebrations with traditional foods — fruity cakes and mulled cider — Yule logs and incense of rosemary, pine and cedar. In Europe there was wassailing, a term which meant drinking and singing in apple orchards. Groves of pine trees were decorated with candles and gifts to the Mother Goddess. Mistletoe and holly honored Zeus and other pagan gods. Native American peoples observed the winter solstice as a time for purification, rituals, retreats, prayerstick making and, occasionally, the last rabbit hunt of the year.

But, dissention is always with us, especially when some of us are having fun, and the winter solstice was not exempt. Its pagan roots blighted Christmas. In Massachusetts in the seventeenth century, the Puritans tried to ban Christmas, saying it was heathenish, and the English Parliament abolished Christmas in 1637. Talk about nothing new under the sun, this was more than 300 years before Dr. Suess wrote about the Grinch who stole Christmas.

Despite this heavy backpack of history and the dark scowl of astrology, I have a different theory about why I'm so sleepy this time of year. I think that somewhere in my family tree there is a furry, hibernating animal. It is genetic — a strong, biological pull toward a hollow tree or a warm cave. My favorite part of Phyllis McGinley's poem *Dissertation on Furniture* is the stanza which begins, "I sing the bed."

I think that these ancient roots of winter holidays and our primitive need to add light to the shortest days of the year have transmuted over the centuries to a modern phenomenon — shopping. First, the frenzied holiday shopping, then more shopping with post-holiday sales. I believe we need all the shopping, celebrating and associated activities — cooking, craft making, card sending, holiday decorating and the other zealous endeavors. We need them to gin up enough energy to keep us going. Otherwise, we all might sing the bed and drift off to hibernating heaven.

Once we reach Twelfth Night, the calendar conclusion of the winter holiday season, we're on the upward climb. January is a month of creature comforts — National Hot Tea Month, National Soup Month and National Oatmeal Month. As a gardener told me, soon it will be February 15 and time to plant potatoes. Then we're on our way to honest-to-goodness spring. From there, it's a straight shot to summer solstice.

BLEEDING HEARTS – A LAMENTATION FOR FERUARY

January gets me down. All that gray, cold, Stockholm weather. When I think I can't get through another day, I go into the garden stores and stare at the rows of spring plants in bloom — tulips, hyacinths and primroses in pastel colors and blossoms as frothy as an old-fashioned Easter bonnet.

By late January, I'm starved for sweetness, for color and scent. Just in the nick of time, there's Valentine season. And poetry. Robert Frost said that poetry is a way of taking life by the throat.

I love love poetry, but I used to love a different kind. I used to love poetry to the height and depth and breadth my soul can reach. Then, Carl Sandburg's *Honey and Salt* and Rod McKuen. But that was back when I thought heartbreak was something chic, like wearing a *Breakfast at Tiffany's* black dress. Once I had my heart broken, I found out there's nothing glamorous about it. It's like being sick in public.

Well, everything changes. Us, too, and if we're lucky, we know it.

I read a long article in *The New York Times* bemoaning the current oh-so-bad roles for men in movies. It seems to me this article appears annually, except every other year it's asking why aren't there any good movie roles for women.

The article was wondering how an entire sex could be portrayed as lacking civility, honor, fidelity, courage and a sense of duty and justice, when suddenly the author cried out — Men no longer barbecue in movies!

What? No longer barbecue in movies?

The article plunged on. Why did men barbecue in the first place, *The New York Times* asked, and then answered its own question. "Because we once lived in a gendered world — outdoors versus indoors, work versus family, hard versus soft ... and when the hearth moved outdoors it moved into male space and thus fell under male control. So men barbecued."

You know, of all the things I brood about, this has never been one of them. Even in February, the month to think about men and love and biology, I don't think I care why men barbecue.

Almost everyone I know is struggling bravely and brightly with heavy loads —serious problems with health or work or insurance or money. They have parents with Alzheimer's, or health problems of their own, or children who abandon their children, or they made wrong turns a couple of decades ago and are now seeking high ground. We're living through a great plague; one friend told me at dinner the other evening that forty-seven of his friends have died of AIDS. We are all, to use Emily Dickinson's phrase, bandaged souls.

The date is the only difference between us and the pioneers who lived on raw, open prairies with enormous distances between them, waiting out the ebony nights. Like them, the best we can do is work and live honorably, build communities, help one another when we're sick, or shot, or trapped in a blizzard, or die in childbirth, or lose our crops, or our home or our cat. We long for pie suppers, picnics and barn dances in the moonlight.

In February, with candy, cards and verse, we celebrate the tide of our heart as it pulls us toward love and romance. Maybe for just this month, we want to believe in simple, storybook ideas: love at first sight, prince charming, girl of my dreams, and happy ever after. We need to know the flower blooms.

As my Februarys stack up, I have learned to appreciate more than one bloom. I can love the whole bouquet and all the colors. I laugh more. I discovered a new book of poetry that fits my current tastes. *Bleeding Hearts — Love Poems for the Nervous and Highly Strung* is an anthology compiled by Michelle Lovric, St. Martin's Press. This book, the cover says, is a collection of tortured poems for the mean times, for the broken hearts, for the trampled hopes, and for the rare and fragile outbreaks of nervous optimism. Some of the poems are red with pain, but most of them are funny and make me laugh.

It reminds me that February is the month of romantic love; no wonder it's the shortest month of the year.

KITH and KIN and CATS

SUDDENLY, FIREFLIES

I have a blurry black-and-white snapshot of me in my first formal gown, about 1956. I'm standing in the back yard; you can see the power lines, the chain-link fence, the neighbor's house, the dog's house and the tall grass. My formal was white net with a sweetheart neckline. I wanted a strapless formal, but it was just too daring, and there was some question about my being able to keep it up. I wore dangling pearl earrings. I thought I had never looked more beautiful. You hardly notice my glasses.

A few years ago I had this photograph made into greeting cards with the caption: *Change can be good.*

I grew up in a dinky Oklahoma town where everybody knew who you were and what you were up to and called your mother and told her. From the time I was a teenager, my goal in life was to get out of that small town and live a life of sophistication in a real city. London, I thought, or New York. Or, as it turned out, Tulsa.

There was a time when Tulsa seemed like London or New York. It was a big city to me. Not only was there more than one movie theatre, there were two daily newspapers, buildings with elevators, and buses. Downtown was crowded with buses. Supper clubs with drinking and dancing were open almost every night. I worked at a television station. You just don't get more cosmopolitan than all of this.

Now I think of Tulsa as a small town and that is one of the things I love about it. I especially love my neighborhood.

My travel agent lives just down the street. She works at home, has a great garden and is slightly eccentric. It can take a while for her to return calls, but that's no problem. If I need to speak to her right away, I call her husband's office and ask him if she is in town or off visiting her grandchildren. The other day I really needed to talk to her, so I left a message saying she had to call me by noon. She did.

"I got your message," she said, "but I can't talk now. I've just come from my therapist and I'm on the way to my acupuncturist." That's the kind of business exchange you can have in a small town. In London or New York, your travel agent would probably say she was "between meetings" or "working on a deadline."

In my wonderfully ordinary neighborhood, children raise money for schools, cheerleading uniforms or musical equipment. They sell candy, cookie dough, gift-wrapping paper. They mow lawns and save the money to buy a car. They solicit underwriters for gymnastic feats. A little girl named Grace, as delicate as a flower fairy, astonished us all by turning ninety-seven somersaults in three minutes.

The neighborhood association sponsors hot dogs and games in the park every spring and a holiday light contest at Christmas.

That is not to say the neighborhood is all pastel and sweet. There is the barking dog, the house with the unsightly front yard and the cranky man who marks off his property with a chalk line and chops down any overhanging leaf or limb from neighboring houses.

One of the things I hated about growing up in a small town was that everyone knew me, and my parents, my aunts and uncles, my friends and all of our histories. I craved anonymity and the freedom that goes with it. People who live in a city, I thought, don't tattle. People who live in a city don't have their mothers come and drag them out of Brigitte Bardot movies.

Now I know the comfort of community. In my neighborhood, we know one another, if not intimately, at least well enough to know if there's a strange car on the block. We know most of the pets up and down the street by name; dogs and cats named Marmalade, Percy and Skeezer. We rescue lost dogs, we search for missing pet rabbits. A fat pug dog named Cleo is recuperating from having a tooth pulled and all sympathize.

An appreciation of small towns and small neighborhoods may be something you have to grow into. To be grateful for small charms, you have to have something to compare them to. Such as overwork and overstress. Ionesco said what brings us together are dreams and anguish.

The Overworked American, a book by Harvard economist Juliet Schor, says that despite the labor-saving promises of science and technology, leisure time is declining. Working hours are on the rise. Since the beginning of the 1990s, every member of the labor force has put in an extra month of work a year.

There was a time when work and career were paramount to me. And there was a time when white formals and pearl earrings were the most important thing in my life. But those sharp interests softened. I changed — sometimes by choice, sometimes less consciously. And with the changes has come a new range of interests: herb gardens, cats, non-fiction and community, which is not the same as social functions.

Twilight is a magical time in the neighborhood.

Front lawns and front porches are littered with lounging cats. A girl rides a bicycle while a big white dog on a leash trots along with her. An older woman with orange hair walks a little orange dog named Foxie. People jogging or watering their lawns wave at one another or stop to chat. A young mother pulls two small children in a red wagon who wave little American flags left over from Memorial Day.

Suddenly — fireflies. As gaudy sunset fades to navy, darkening lawns begin to twinkle. The whole neighborhood sparkles.

FAMILY VACATIONS

I read an article in *The New York Times* about a different kind of family holiday. Instead of going over the river and through the woods to grandmother's house for a big dinner, whole extended families go to a resort. Sometimes it's great. Other times, siblings discover they have packed all their cares and woes of a lifetime, hyped with holiday expectations, and they're unloading them somewhere expensive and isolated where they can't get away from one another.

Just another way we're not like the oyster. With humans, a little irritant, perfected for twenty or thirty years, usually doesn't turn into a pearl.

Although I had read the article and grasped the information, I ignored the warnings. That summer, for the first time, my sister, my mother, my niece and I took a trip together. We made these plans in a high flush of bonding. Then my sister and I began to remember all those summer vacations as children, not to mention little get-togethers of recent years; by the time we set off on this trip, we had about the same enthusiasm we had when we lined up for polio shots in grade school.

We all met in Tucson and drove through the Sonoran Desert, which, thanks to El Niño and record rainfalls, bloomed blue and yellow with wildflowers. That seemed like a good omen. We were headed for Puerto Peñasco, an old shrimp-fishing village in Mexico. We would share a condominium and relax — nothing to do but walk on the white beach and look at the aqua waters of the Sea of Cortez.

We had not been there ten minutes when one of the bathrooms flooded, the screen door fell off the patio and the landlord disappeared for the weekend. So, now that the accommodations were settled, we could concentrate on just being together as a family.

At night we played cards. Well, some of us did. Remember the movie *The Cincinnati Kid* about high stakes card games with Joan Blondell as the dealer named Lady Fingers? That could have been my mother. My mother must know a hundred card games but the gene seems to skip generations. My niece, the sainted granddaughter, is the only person I know who can play cards like a machine and chatter without taking a breath. It's as if her brain and her hands work in two parts.

My sister wouldn't play at all. I tried to be a good sport and play, but I can never remember how many cards to deal.

"Did I play first the last hand?" I asked.

"Yes," my mother said sweetly, "you played first and very badly."

My sister Candee is younger than I am, and she claims that I say she is brassy and loud. I would never say that. Although she is social. Very social.

She says I sleep all the time, which is not true.

One day in Mexico, my sister's friend Mary Carol came to lounge in the sun with us. Mary Carol's older sister had been to visit her the week before. I was dozing in the sun, listening to them talk and thinking about little sisters.

Little sisters all have names like Candee and Mary Carol. They all have curly hair and dimples. They were all cheerleaders. They're all social. They're chummy with waiters, they talk to everybody. In Mexico, my sister went out for every meal — twice. The meal was in one place, dessert was at another. One evening she took us to still a third place where she and my mother danced the macarena at Manny's Beach Club. Dancing is another thing little sisters do, anything aerobic and hopping.

So, this drowsy afternoon, my mother and niece were inside playing cards and talking and talking and talking. I was lying in the shade, and the two little sisters were sitting in the sun carrying on a strange conversation.

"Does she have platinum earrings?" one would say.

"No, but she's got a gold watch from Tiffany's. That counts."

They seemed to be talking about me, but speaking in a strange verb tense — third person invisible.

"Does she drink espresso?"

"Even better — café latte. That's one for me."

Then they began to talk to me, but all in questions, a kind of anthropological survey.

"Do you own a pair of denim pants? Do you have canvas shoes? What brand? Do you shop at Neiman's? Saks?"

Eventually they wandered off to look at the flooding bathroom and when they went through my bedroom they burst into laughter. Great rounds of laughter rolled down the hall.

They came out onto the patio on wheels of laughter.

"We saw your socks," my sister laughed. "Little pink anklets with lace. Thank you. That put me over the top. I won the fluffy sister contest."

Fluffy Sister Contest. That's the kind of thing little sisters do to amuse one another.

A couple of days later we drove home. My niece and mother sat in the backseat. Without a fan of cards in their hands, they seemed stunned into silence. Then, suddenly, they would burst into conversation, like characters from the Robin Williams' movie *Awakenings*. They would sit quietly until something set them off, some word like *chalupa* or some sight like an ice cream store sign, and then the would talk at the same time, words as fast and blurred as a dog race.

My sister thought some music would be nice on the drive home. I suggested Vivaldi, that's lively and festive. But it was her car and her CD's, so what we got was Spanish disco music. Four hours of Spanish disco music. I took a nap and dreamed about desert wildflowers dancing the macarena and singing about tequila.

We have talked about the trip several times since I got home and we agree; all in all, it went better than we thought it would. A lot better. We're already thinking about the next trip. There's nothing like family is there?

FLAG DAY

From May through July, summer is the season of flags: Armed Forces Day, Memorial Day, Flag Day, Fourth of July.

Beyond being colorful and festive, a fluttering flag stirs powerful emotions. The colors of the United States flag are rich with symbolism: red is the symbol of daring, white is for purity, and blue signifies the nation's covenant against oppression, which was an inspiration from Scotland. The stars represent a new constellation rising in the west.

Flags always remind me of the VFW in my hometown in northeast Oklahoma. The VFW hosted turkey shoots, horse races, bingo parties and patriotic celebrations. When I was a teenager, rock-and-roll dances were held at the VFW every Saturday night. The next morning the boys tried to recall Homeric fights in the parking lot and checked to see how many bruises or broken bones they had. That's how they measured what a good time they had.

But I'm thinking of an earlier period, the 1950s. For a while there was a Civil Defense program at the VFW to spot enemy aircraft. My parents were good citizens, patriotic and community-minded. My father was a proud veteran, a Mason and a volunteer fireman; my mother was a homeroom mother at my grade school, dutiful with plates of cookies and cupcakes. She made an angel food cake with butter icing for the cakewalk at the annual school carnival. In the small town version of a barn-raising, my parents and their friends would rally together and, in a flurry of activity, knock off ambitious projects: building a storm shelter, laying a hardwood floor or making a tubful of homemade tamales.

So, my parents signed up for the Civil Defense aircraft program. There was a training session, then they were assigned to a shift. Every week for months each of them went to the VFW for an hour-long shift. They climbed the aircraft-spotting tower built especially for the purpose and spent an hour scanning the skies with binoculars for enemy planes. It went without saying that they would be Russian planes. This was the Cold War.

Today I realize that if enemy aircraft had got as far inland as Oklahoma without being spotted, our country would have been in deep trouble. But we didn't think about that then. It was the community spirit that counted.

Part of the Civil Defense assignment was to record the time and type of each airplane sighted. My parents never spotted any Russian planes, but they did see quite a few aircraft headed toward the Tulsa airport. My mother had such poor eyesight that she couldn't identify the planes. She wrote down the time and recorded each plane as "unidentified.'

About that time, my Uncle Bus, who is a worrier by nature, was suffering sleepless nights worrying about a Russian attack. I told this story to a young friend of mine not long ago, a Russian ballet dancer from St. Petersburg. He was puzzled.

"Your uncle worry that Russians come over here?" he asked. "Well, he was right. Here I am."

I'm pretty sure my uncle didn't lie awake nights on an Oklahoma farm worrying about an invasion of Russian ballet dancers. Ah, the Cold War. You really had to be there.

Despite the fear and paranoia, and the ludicrousness, there's a sweetness to this story about the Civil Defense tower at the VFW. I have a wonderful image of my pretty mother in the tower, wearing a crisp sundress, squinting intently at the summer skies through her horn-rimmed glasses. There was a sense of community spirit, not for social recognition or business profit, just for the good of the community and the family. Maybe that's what kept the enemy at bay.

A WHEEL FALLS OFF

You know those times you're just tootin' along and suddenly a wheel falls off of your life? That's what my life has been like lately.

First I caught a sinus infection that lasted for weeks and left me staggering around at half speed and in a weakened condition.

Then my cat got critically ill. Emergency room, hospitalization. Serious stuff.

And then my mother got critically ill. Emergency room, hospitalization. Serious stuff.

I've been learning words that slide into your life like serpents and slice you up like stilettos, words like hypertrophic cardiomyopathy and multiple myeloma. Suddenly, the whole world seemed like a dark Rilke poem: "Everything was close to my face and everything close to my face was stone."

My emotional responses are out of sync. I can be very calm during the big stuff, but fly into an instant rage over something trifling like a rude driver or an officious secretary. Then, unexpectedly, at the sight of a crescent moon or the peace of a yoga class, I burst into tears of grief.

I don't know that there's a happy ending to this story, but there's a happy continuing chapter. And it's because of my friends, friends who talk to me about it, and who leave care packages at my door: parcels of ripe pears, pastries, lavender bath salts, chocolate and red wine. Comfort items that really work.

Most of the time they don't leave a note, don't even

sign their name. They don't have to. I know who they are. They're the friends who are also struggling with some of life's knocks: sick parents or siblings or children with bipolar disease, diabetes, strokes, Alzheimer's and trying to resolve problems with health care, transportation and nursing homes.

I began to think of us as a group of adults going through life like very small children on an outing, each holding a knot in a rope and trying to look out for the kids around us. Sharing a cookie maybe or pointing out a great big bug on the sidewalk.

It's my friends who are helping me put this wheel back on.

Yet not everything is kind and nurturing. Just when I needed the most pampering, I got one of the worst haircuts of my life. I look exactly like Gertrude Stein. I am so angry. And so ugly.

One of my friends who is going through a Buddhist stage told me these things are sent to remind me that (1) nothing is permanent and (2) I'm not in control of anything. I thought about those lessons while I dressed for a meeting, putting on a tunic with a lot of Chinese knot buttons, little cloth things that are onerous to fasten. I struggled and struggled with them, then stepped back to admire myself. I had buttoned the whole blouse crooked. I burst out laughing. Not in control? Are you kidding. I can't even get my clothes on straight.

A lesson I *have* learned is the urgency of Doing It Now. Whatever is important to you, do it now. Brush the cat, take your mother to lunch, write the book, sit in the garden.

In the midst of all this heavy stuff, the first daffodil bloomed in my yard, the first daffodil of spring. What faith.

"Ah, yes," a friend said, "now it's time to plant lettuce."

"And keep your eyes on the daffodils," another friend said. "They know something."

AUNTS AND UNCLES

The summer my Aunt Helen died, I lost a heroine. In my hometown, she had been a telephone operator for twenty years in an era when you spoke to the operator and told her the phone number you wanted to call. The telephone office was up some rickety stairs on a second floor and during tornado season, when the rest of the town was in storm cellars, valiant Aunt Helen was up there by herself, keeping in touch with the sheriff's department and tracking the storm's progress

Aunt Helen was my role model, not just because she was a working woman in the 1950s, but because she taught me how to make potato soup and loaned me her Book of the Month Club selections. That's pretty heady stuff when you're ten or twelve.

Every Sunday the whole family — all my aunts and uncles and cousins — gathered at my grandmother's house for Sunday dinner. The main course was usually fried chicken, grabbed from my grandmother's chicken coop that morning, and strawberry shortcake, with strawberries my grandmother and I had picked from her strawberry patch the day before.

It was an old-fashioned family. The men ate first and then the women. A separate table for children was in the kitchen. My mother was more progressive, and when the family dinners moved to our house years later, she changed this antiquated ritual and everybody ate together.

For Aunt Helen's funeral, the elderly relatives fell back into the old pattern. The aunts rode together in my car on the way to the family plot on the Kansas prairie, and the uncles kept to themselves.

I know this family cemetery plot well. When I was a girl, Decoration Day was a big holiday. For weeks the aunts would make crepe paper roses, wax them and assemble them into wreaths. Decorating the family graves was a big outing. As my cousins and I grew up, we forsook this ritual. The aunts looked at us with disappointment, then disgust, and finally, they just ignored us.

The family has shrunk now. The great-aunts and uncles are gone. When Aunt Helen died, what's left of us were there in August for her burial in the Kansas cemetery. The temperature was 103 degrees; it had been a record heat wave and drought. Suddenly, in the middle of the funeral, the skies opened with a pounding rainstorm. It was the storm scene from *King Lear*. Men hung onto the funeral tent to keep it from blowing away. As the winds grew and galed, the men leaned with their whole weight into the tent poles.

The minister never faltered. He raised his voice over the din of the storm and kept sermonizing in a loud voice about the Twenty-third Psalm, David and Absolom. Then, another danger loomed. The tent sagged with gallons of rainwater and threatened to collapse on us. Strong men wrestled with the canvas, heaved it upward and saved the day by sending the water gushing off the tent. Unfortunately, this water cascaded onto a poor cousin who was standing under it. Now he was as wet as I was after my dash to roll up the car windows.

The excitement was not over yet. Just as the storm raced away over the prairies, the mechanism holding the casket gave way and sent the coffin plunging into the earth. Burly funeral employees appeared and hand-cranked it back to the surface, puffing and murmuring under their breaths.

The younger among us had run and cowered and fought with tents and cranks, but the aging aunts and uncles had not moved from their seats on the front rows. They had watched the action with keen interest as if it were part of the ceremony. And they weren't ready to leave yet.

They creaked to their feet and hobbled around the family plot examining their own gravestones and showing them to one another. Their headstones were engraved with maiden names and military records, everything but the final date, already in place for the big day.

I was distracted from all of these plans for eternal rest by problems with my car. It had begun making horrible grinding noises on the way to the cemetery. The uncles and I raised the hood and peered in. We got down on our knees and looked under the car. The uncles are in their element around vehicles. They had spent a lot of time during those Sunday family dinners out in the garage or gathered around cars and pickups. If it were a holiday, there was often a whiskey bottle in a brown bag hidden in a trunk of one of those vehicles. The uncles' holiday moods grew cheerier as the day progressed.

The uncles agreed that the car sounded pretty serious. Universal joint, or transmission, they said. It was so serious, they broke rank and one of the uncles rode in the women's car on the trip home. Every time the car groaned he nodded happily in affirmation.

"Uh huh," he'd say, "there it is. That's it."

Eventually, the aunts and uncles were deposited at their homes and I set out by myself for the final leg to Tulsa.

My hair was wet and my dress was wet. I had had an allergic reaction to the prairie wind and one eye was swelling shut. My car was lurching and grinding.

The last thing an uncle said before I drove away was, "Now be careful because that thing could go out at any minute and throw the whole car right into the oncoming traffic."

I've never seen so many big trucks on the highway. With every approaching one, I'd clutch the wheel, hold my breath and wonder, "Is this it?"

Because, as one of the aunts always says, "Life's funny, isn't it?"

GARDEN PARTY

It was reading F. Scott Fitzgerald as a young woman that created for me an indelible image of the romantic party.

First I read *Tender is the Night* and later I read about the couple who were Fitzgerald's inspiration for the novel. Calvin Tompkins wrote about Sara and Gerald Murphy and their life on the Riviera in the 1920s in *Living Well is the Best Revenge*, a book as slim and elegant as they were. Their world, it seemed to me in northeast Oklahoma, was one of ultimate glamour. Their champagne and caviar parties included such guests as Ernest Hemingway, Scott and Zelda Fitzgerald, Pablo Picasso, and artists of the Diaghilev Ballet; it was a time and place that glittered, dazzled and charmed. The center of this intoxicating world was the Murphy's French villa and its garden, fragrant with oleander, mimosa, jasmine and heliotrope. "At night," Tompkins wrote, "the whole place throbbed with nightingales."

One recent summer evening, I went to a garden party almost that evocative. Granted, it was in Tulsa, not in the south of France, but it was an enchanting party. It began in a lingering summer twilight as mockingbirds ran through their musical repertoire and mourning doves cooed. The evening air was scented with peonies, iris, roses and honeysuckle.

The party spilled outside onto the patio. Silver coolers of iced champagne misted over. Tables held platters of smoked salmon, pink and thinly sliced, and sideboards were lined with silver trays heaped with petit fours and tiny cream puffs.

As lovely as this setting was, the soul of the party was the guests — about twenty people threaded together by interests in music and books. A sense of festivity hung in the air, as everyone seemed ready to throw off the routine of winter. It was early summer, time to shuck the heavy work mode and put on a mood that was light and sheer and caught the breeze.

The fizz of the party was its purpose — to celebrate the birthday of a cat. There was to be a little musicale, a program of guests singing and playing the piano (music from *CATS,* of course) and poetry recitation (T.S. Eliot's *Old Possom's Book of Practical Cats.*) Everyone was delighted by the whimsy that set this tone. The evening was gentle and playful.

It was an adult party with only two little boys in attendance. Mostly they ran in feverish circles around the garden, whizzing past the stately iris.

The program began with the host reading a poem in a polished, theatrical voice. One of the little boys had come inside and stood looking up at this oddity. It was a Norman Rockwell scene; the little boy, perhaps six years old, in short pants and a striped t-shirt, statue-still and gazing up at the tall, stately man reading poetry in a rich baritone. When the man paused to turn the pages to a second selection, the little boy stepped forward and tugged at the man's arm. The man looked down at him politely and we all leaned forward to hear what the little boy would say. Something in childlike admiration, we knew, something in innocent amazement.

The little boy's brave, piping voice rang through the room. "Is there cake?" he asked.

The audience burst into laughter, the hostess hurried away to set out the cat's birthday cake for the little boys, and the program continued, happier for the interruption.

That question should be a bumper sticker, a needlepoint pillow or calligraphy framed on the wall. I love it because it is philosophical, pragmatic, hopeful, direct yet enigmatic. It's what we all want to know, isn't it?

It is a better way of asking the questions about life's tedium: Is this going to go on forever? Is this worth my time? Is there any reward? Is there a payoff to this job? Does this have a happy ending?

All of those questions are wrapped up in that one, simple, beautiful question as plain as a child can express it. It applies to almost anything in life. What better way to ask it: Is there cake?

UNFUNNY SHAGGY DOG STORY

Along with the wisdom that comes with getting older is the tendency to be less judgmental. I read this in a book titled *You're Not Old Until You're 90.* Even if it's not universally true, I think it's good advice.

There are a lot of things out there that are not for me, but which are genuine passions for other people: kick boxing and body piercing, spelunking and string bikinis. The list is very long.

When it comes to pets, I don't mean to denigrate the more exotic pets such as iguanas or gerbils, but they are not for me. I did have white rats once, but not exactly as pets. In high school a couple of us had a science project with rats and nutrition and we named the rats after our friends — Pauline, Martha, Shirley and Judy, which our friends did not take as a compliment.

Among those of us who are slaves to pets, I think there are dog people and cat people, with few crossovers. I like dogs, except those big, snarly, jumpy ones, but I am definitely a cat person and I seem to grow cattier every year.

Recently I was visiting an animal clinic crammed with dogs and cats for adoption. The veterinarian looked exhausted.

"What can I do to help?" I asked.

"Would you foster a pregnant cat?" she asked. She had rescued it from the animal shelter. The little pregnant calico was long-legged, underfed and thin, except for the round belly full of babies. She was in a cage surrounded by caged, barking dogs and I thought she deserved a better place than that to give birth.

So that is how I came to transform my garage quarters into the Cronley Home for Unwed Cats. I cleaned it and moved out boxes so that it was uncrowded; she would need space for exercise. I rearranged furniture so there were places at the windows for her to rest and look out. A window, I believe, is a cat's version of novel-and-television entertainment. The quarters seemed damp, so I bought a new dehumidifier. And a new litter box because an expectant mother deserves that, I reasoned.

I called the cat Lola. Big mistake to name her, right? She arrived, inspected the box lined with towels I had arranged for her, and twenty-four hours later, while I was inside having a nap, she had her kittens. Five wiggly baby kittens. I tried hard not to name them. Except for the pudgy orange-and-white one I called Orange Julius, the spunky female I dubbed Cordelia, and the gray tiger-striped kitten I addressed as William Blake.

When Lola developed a cough I panicked. What if she got really sick? What if she didn't produce milk? What about the five babies? Would they starve to death? I raced to get medication for her. For a couple of days I was on my hands and knees, spoon-feeding her nutritious baby food. When I had to go out of town, I hired a professional pet nanny to look after her and the kittens. Lola is well now and I'm feeling a lot better myself.

So with that behavioral history, it was incomprehensible to hear the story of an elderly woman who went into the hospital to have surgery and came home to discover that her daughter had got rid of her two cats.

I have repeated this story with horror, and, what's

even more horrible, almost everyone I tell it to has a similar story. The happy, shaggy dog taken to the animal shelter because the owner was tired of it; the cats who were turned out onto the street when the owner died; the healthy Pekingese taken to a vet to be euthanized because the owner was going into a nursing home; the five beautiful Persian cats taken to the animal shelter because the pet store was going out of business.

Well, surely there are more details to these stories than I know but although it's judgmental, I can't think of any that matter. There are alternatives.

I have an electric mixer that's thirty-five years old and broken; I'm trying to get repaired because I try not to contribute to a throwaway, disposable society. So I can't understand people who feel that living animals are as dispensable as used razors or weak batteries. I'm polishing a theory that how we care for our weakest, most defenseless unit is the real measure of our society.

Millions of dogs and cats in animal shelters across the country are killed every year because pet owners are irresponsible. They don't have the pets neutered, they don't accept permanent responsibility.

The local animal shelter kills about 14,000 dogs and cats a year. It is a good shelter and works to encourage pet adoption and foster care for kittens and puppies. The veterinarians and animal rescue organizations I know are doing heroic work to promote neutering and spaying of dogs and cats and to find permanent, caring homes for homeless dogs and cats. Obviously a lot of educational work needs to be done with the other animals — the pets' owners.

All of the animal rescue organizations need help,

especially volunteers and funds. We have a long way to go before this shaggy dog story has a happy ending.

CAT LOVERS

This is the story of how I discovered my inner cat.

One upon a time, many cats ago, there were no cats at all in my life. This was B.P. — Before Phoebe. Phoebe is the gregarious, calico Manx who taught me that I am a cat person.

Here is my observation about pet owners.

Dog people are dedicated to their pets, but cat people are passionate about cats.

Dog people are energetic folks, given to athletics, hearty meals and Garth Brooks.

Cat people are quiet, creative people who like gardening, cups of tea and good books.

Authors who have written about cats include Colette, Baudelaire, Rudyard Kipling, Pablo Neruda, Saki, May Sarton, Thoreau, P.G. Wodehouse and Emile Zola.

Mark Twain said, "If mankind could be crossed with the cat, it would improve mankind but deteriorate the cat."

Cat people are fanciful, too. A couple I know gave a birthday party for their cat, Topaz, a tabby with aquamarine eyes. It was an elegant evening with lovely refreshments and musical entertainment. The cat of honor chose not to come out from under the bed.

Cats in a home dictate furniture placement. The general rule is: Something by every window, so that every room is a room with a view.

Also, something tall to climb for a lofty perspective of the world, and something low to hide under when the world is looking for you. Not a bad philosophy for all of us animals.

I eased into the tide of those making cats the No. 1 pet in America. First, I had one cat, one perfect cat. But Phoebe was lonely while I was at work, and that meant mischief.

The solution, my cat friends said, was to get a cat for Phoebe. It worked. Phoebe and Abigail were inseparable companions, and so I had two perfect calico cats.

Then, when neighbors moved, I adopted Midnight, a male black-and-white tuxedo cat. "It'll never work," skeptics said. "They'll never get along." But it did work, it just took patience. Cats can teach us lessons we need to learn. Such as patience.

After I had met my personal quota of cats, I began acquiring cats by accident. One day in my back yard, I rescued a homeless cat that fell starving into my arms. I was so naïve I thought someone would rush over, congratulate me for being a fine citizen and take the cat away to a good home. Every animal organization I called was full.

That is how I got involved as a volunteer with StreetCats, a nonprofit adoption agency for rescuing, inoculating, neutering and placing homeless cats in permanent homes. It is one of several Tulsa animal rescue organizations working for a humane solution to the problem of the city's homeless animals.

Even before this, I had firsthand experience in the joys of secondhand cats. I was working for an arts organization when the staff and I found an orange cat living under the building. We thought he was a kitten, but he turned out to be a malnourished, mature cat about ten years old.

We adopted him, named him Stagedoor Johnny and paid for his vet bills and food. We loved him. Having an office cat to pet and hold was great for relieving stress. During breaks the frazzled rehearsal pianist would dash in and say, "Quick. I need a cat fix." She walked up and down the hall hugging Johnny and whispering to him. I'm sure they exchanged musical secrets.

Stagedoor Johnny became a minor celebrity. He was as temperamental as any artist I've ever known. He could be a cranky cat. On cold, damp days, his joints seemed to ache and when we picked him up, he was likely to hiss or nip us lightly. We understood. Some days we wanted to hiss at people, too.

His favorite occupation was to lie near the rehearsal room and doze to the sound of the music, a testimonial to the power of music to soothe the beast in all of us.

Yet with any audience, Stagedoor Johnny turned on the charm. Children could sit on the floor and pet him for hours and he would purr patiently. He regularly snarled at the doting staff, but he never raised a whisker to a guest. He was a valuable public relations expert, and good at his job.

After several years, the aging cat retired into private life with people who adored him.

I have never been in deeper grief than when my cat Abigail died. It was a grief like a well, and people who understood consoled me as if I'd lost a member of the family, which I had. Phoebe grieved too.

Eventually I took my own advice and adopted an adult cat from StreetCats.

Sophie was almost lifeless when she was rescued, an undersized, underfed mother of four. Her tail had been bobbed by some trauma. The four kittens were adopted right away, but nobody wanted Sophie. Except StreetCats. And then, me.

She was so happy to have a home of her own, there wasn't even a period of adjustment. Within minutes she was exploring the house. Then she sat on the kitchen counter watching me make gingerbread.

Sophie has blossomed in her new home, growing playful and plump. We are both grateful to StreetCats.

According to the International Society for Animal Rights, "The caring people in shelters are not killing animals because they want to. They are forced to because of the irresponsibility of owners who cause the tragedy."

We can all be part of the solution. Neuter your pet. Support animal rescue organizations with your time, talent and funds. If you can, adopt a pet. Kindness and caring will help the cats and dogs and will improve our own species.

OH, THOSE FRENCH WOMEN

To celebrate our graduation from college some thirty years ago, my friend Michele and I went to Paris. We went with our new journalism degrees in hand, our eyes shining with sky-high futures and our heads full of tender hopes of getting jobs at the *Paris Herald-Tribune*.

We dressed for the flight, wore our best clothes and heels, of course. I wore a pale turquoise suit, which was so dirty by the time I got there that I sent it out to be cleaned and didn't see it again for three weeks, just in time for the return flight home. A beau had given me roses as I left and I carried that white box of long-stemmed red roses all the way to Paris. As you can imagine, upon arrival the roses didn't look any better than the turquoise suit.

Michele and I spoke little French and that badly. We stayed at a *pension* where we could never make ourselves understood at the cafeteria. The only words we could communicate to the servers were *poulet* and *chocolat*. We damn neared starved, but luckily chicken and hot chocolate were on the menu frequently. I learned later that the servers were Spanish and they couldn't speak French either.

The Vietnam War was daily television news and because of their history in Indochina, the French seemed to despise Americans in general and Michele and me in particular. Otherwise, surely one person in the whole of Paris would have understood us in the Metro when we asked directions. We walked a lot, equally conscientious about sightseeing and our image. We always wore dresses and heels. We walked for miles every day in heels.

When our trip ended, I came back to Tulsa, but Michele stayed, married a Frenchman, raised a family and has lived in Paris ever since. In the spring of 1998, I returned to Paris for the first time to visit her and the city of my cornfed, youthful dreams.

"I don't want to see just tourist things," I told her, "I want to see what it's like to live in Paris." Mostly, that life seems to be centered on shopping for food, but that's the story of the gourmet and gourmand French and their quest for the freshest and finest foodstuffs.

Buying bread is a daily routine because the *baguette* is designed to be fresh and edible for only twelve hours. Bread is an art form in France, with an ancient history. The first *école de boulangerie* was established in Paris in 1780. The bread-baking artisans have not one but two patron saints, Saint Honoré and Saint Roche.

The open-air market in Michele's fashionable neighborhood was crowded with stalls of fresh meats, fish, flowers, olives, salads, lavender, table linen and fruit, but none was more appealing than the cheese stall. The smell of fresh *fromage* beckoned from a lavish assortment of cheeses in every shape, size and texture, and in colors ranging from creamy white to dark gold. Still, this bountiful display was only a sampling of the 300 to 500 cheeses produced in France. As we shopped, Michele whispered to me the etiquette of cheese buying. Indicate, gesture or point to the cheese you want to sample or buy; never, ever touch the cheese, as I was prone to do. They were so alluring — and some as plump as Pillsbury Doughboys — that I wanted to poke them.

In this country we might quip that someone we

consider dim is "no rocket scientist." At the French market, they might ask, "He thinks he invented the wire that cuts cheese?" Here, a salesclerk might hope we have a nice day. At the open-air market, the tradesmen say thank you and goodbye with the phrase, "To your good heart."

As preparation for my French immersion, a Belgian friend gave me a book titled *French or Foe?*, an insider's guidebook to bridging the cultural differences and to communicating effectively (and nonverbally) with the French. There is advice for dealing with French families, in-laws, schools, strangers, tradespeople, bureaucracy, dinner parties and more. The book interprets French history, culture, space and time and our American difficulty in navigating with grace through those subjects.

The book helped me enormously, at least the half I read on the way over. I read the other half on the flight home, mortified at the unconscious gaucheries I had committed, such as cutting off the tip of Brie cheese. *Quel horreur*! These are the things that mark us as barbarians to the reserved French.

The riddle of the French culture is not new. In the early 1900s, when she was living in Paris, Edith Wharton wrote a book about it. She observed that we Americans are "a pioneer people destined to experiment in new social conditions." The French, by contrast, are identified by qualities of reverence and continuity. That's what comes from being surrounded by 2,000 years of history. The reason streets and Metro stops are named for German cites, for example, is to commemorate Napoleon's greatest victories. To me, something really old is a 1958 Chevy. The French still glory in the twelfth century.

The most important lesson I learned in my reading about French culture was about smiling. Or, more accurately, not smiling. In this part of America, we smile a lot. It means we're friendly, open and welcoming. It's different in France. The French don't smile at people they don't know. They don't smile without a reason. To do so seems hypocritical to them, perhaps even simple-minded.

Another French quality I learned to appreciate is quietness. At home and in public, the French speak softly and quietly to one another. The Parisians I met were reserved; they don't take up much personal space. They don't laugh loudly. Maybe in a crowded city, this wraps individuals in a quiet privacy. In Paris, to prevent noise pollution, it's against the law to honk your car horn.

The third quality is one of such importance, but so common, I probably would have missed it had it not been spelled out to me in the book. It is the polite ritual of greeting. Every transaction — with the postman, the taxi driver, the shop clerk, the neighbor in the elevator — begins with a polite greeting: *Bonjour monsieur* or *bonjour madame*. Every transaction concludes with the equivalent of *au revoire*. Among acquaintances, there is also a handshake. I saw little boys about ten years old stop their bicycles and exchange *bonjours* and handshakes.

When foreigners fail to politely greet the salesperson or bureaucrat, the breach of etiquette can result in a difficult transaction. Then we say the French are rude. In truth, they were offended because our behavior has been the equivalent of snapping our fingers and bawling out, "Hey you."

All of this brings me to the French women. The

classic French woman seems to personify the nation's cultural philosophy. I saw women shopping, walking down the street, dining out, appearing on television and in their own homes, but whatever the situation, everything about them seemed chic. They had clean faces with understated makeup. They wore smooth hair, brushed back and unfussy. Their clothes were simple and tailored — usually for daytime, a skirt, a plain t-shirt and a little sweater over their shoulders. Often, they wore *le foulard* — a scarf. Except in the hottest weather, Michele explained to me, no fashionable French woman would leave home without a scarf. A scarf at the throat suggests a sensible care for one's health and it completes the look, much as a man in a suit wears a necktie. The weather was warm and most of the French women I saw wore skirts with bare, shiny legs that had been waxed professionally. Their faces were animated but unsmiling.

Think of Catherine Denueve: cool, quiet, serene, poised and floating through life like a swan. That is the quintessential French woman.

I once saw Joanne Woodward say on a television show that she was so nervous when she had to appear as herself that she pretended she was Lauren Bacall. That's how I tried on these three French qualities — polite, quiet and reserved. I pretended I was Catherine Denueve. And you know, I think it worked. Even wearing jeans and with nursery room French, I got along fine in Paris and never saw any of the notoriously prickly French personality I'd heard about.

Then, again, my friend told me that everybody in France had been told over and over to be on their best behavior and to be nice to visitors because the World Cup was approaching and the city would be full of foreign tourists. So maybe it was just lucky timing.

I accepted my good fortune serenely, with the barest hint of a smile.

PARENTAL LESSONS

There are a lot of books on the subject of caring for elderly or ill parents and I wish to heaven I'd read some of them. Or paid more attention to my friends when they talked about home care, hospitals and assisted living.

Mostly my approach has been to hold my breath and try to tiptoe past the subject. One day I found that I was one of them — an adult daughter of a mother who is ill and needing help, but determined to go her own way and resist most of my suggestions, from diet to medical treatment.

This is nothing new until it happens to you and then it's as if you woke up on Jupiter and don't understand the language, not even sign language. Faraway siblings suddenly seem to be alien beings. They swoop in like Luke Skywalker determined to save the day, then fly away home. From there they give lots of long-distance advice. They're probably frustrated by the space and feeling helpless. A lot of their communications seems to begin with "What you need to do ..."

On the home front, elderly or ill parents need lots of things: medical care, better nutrition, a safe environment, transportation, someone to mow the lawn and some semblance of independence and self-esteem.

Well, don't we all, but this is help that's not easy to give or to receive. Except the lawn mowing part.

I'm not talking about big situations, when hospitalization or assisted living is the clear solution. I mean that long, gray space between now and then, the declines and rallies, the tug of war over responsibility, the eggshell path of help and wisdom. It is a wobbly dance forward and back, with detours to the side and all the cha cha cha that comes with families.

So far here's what I've learned:

1. What looks like the solution, isn't always.
2. Easy answers are more difficult than we realize.
3. We don't always learn things the first time.
4. Old patterns have deep roots.
5. It's easier to give advice than to take it.
6. Other people may not take or agree with our advice.
7. They may be wrong.
8. We may be wrong.
9. We believe what we want to believe.
10. It's harder to lose weight than it used to be.

Number ten is a bonus and doesn't have anything to do with caring for elderly people, but right now I'm grateful for any nugget of wisdom that comes my way.

THE METAPHOR OF THE GUEST

In the middle of the summer, I went to Canada. I thought of it as much more dramatic than "going to Canada." It was July and 100 degrees and I thought of it as being snatched from the teeth of a brutal heat wave.

I was a guest at a place far from my daily life — a cottage on Lake Joseph, north of Toronto. It is a land of forests, clear lakes and the great, rocky soil of the Canadian Shield. This is a place and lifestyle that I had never seen, the Canadian version of going to Grand Lake. There were some similarities, such as too many noisy, personal water vehicles for my taste, but much of visiting Lake Joseph was like going back in time. At night, we went across the lake in an antique powerboat to dine at the Country Club. The boat was all polished wood, built in 1927 as a lady's boat for the lady of the house, who was my hostess's grandmother. Dinner at the Country Club — the dècor, the dress, the reserved behavior — was a lot like the 1950s.

What the Canadians call cottages are large, airy houses, often seventy years old or older. Our cottage was an old farmhouse with five bedrooms, high ceilings, painted floors and screened porches the width of the house. The downstairs porch was furnished with hammocks, wicker chairs and a table for supper. Directly overhead was a screened-in sleeping porch. Nearby was a guest cottage the size of most Oklahoma ranch-style houses and, at the water's edge, a boathouse with living accommodations like a big apartment.

Midday, we swam in the lake, but at night we needed comforters on the beds. Early in the morning, with dew on the grass like gaudy rhinestones, we picked raspberries in the garden. About five o'clock in the evening, we had tea on the lawn with bowls of fresh raspberries, cold lobster, bread and butter. Later, everyone gathered in the cavernous kitchen to make supper. One guest had arrived in a turn-of-the-century steamboat. It took two baskets of wood, he said, to get up enough steam to make the trip across the lake and back. He took us for a spin around the lake's edge and as we putt-putted along, shielded by the boat's striped awning, I felt we were in a scene from *The African Queen*. One evening, a bishop and his wife came to tea.

Even with all this memorable activity, the most extraordinary part of my trip was being a guest of people who make hosting artful and gracious.

Being a guest meant I was given the seat with the best view of the lake. I was served first and urged to ride in the front seat of the car or boat. At breakfast they handed me the newspaper arts sections they had saved for me. When local guests came for drinks, I was pulled into the conversation, introduced with such descriptive praise that I barely recognized myself and was urged to tell some of my best stories.

My Canadian hosts, Hilary and Ann, had been friends from their schooldays. They planned activities to delight me. A little shop they knew I would like. The McMichael Museum so I could see the Group of Seven Canadian painters. An Indian artist's studio with native crafts of bark and quill. They had seen and done these things dozens of times, but they made them seem like adventures. "It's such fun to show you this stuff," they said, "to show you where we come from, because when you see it, we see it with new eyes."

What feels so special about being a guest is the sense of being chosen, singled out, for special treatment. With this sensation, the new place gleamed like a wrapped gift.

It made me aware of the art of caring. It made me aware of being grateful. Grateful to be cared for. Conscious that time was limited and precious.

The University of Tulsa has a high-quality faculty with many extraordinary professors. One of TU's greatest professors was Winston Weathers, a writer and a literature professor. He is retired now but still spoken of with reverence for his intellect, his teaching and his writing. He was always considered a gentleman of letters.

Back in the 1970s when demonstrations erupted on college campuses, even conservative TU felt some of the ripples of unrest. Dr. Weathers wrote an essay titled *Meditations in an Empty Classroom*. One of the themes was the question of whose campus is it. He alluded to Emily Dickinson and the metaphor of the guest.

Maybe none of us is the owner, he suggested: "Maybe wisdom is the host and we're all guests. And as guests, we should mind our manners and be on our best behavior."

I remembered that when I was at Lake Joseph in Canada. It is such a graceful way to spend the summer. And, come to think of it, the rest of the year. Drinking more tea. Reading more Emily Dickinson. Minding our manners and being on our best behavior.

JOURNEYS

One Sunday not long ago I put my mother on a plane to Tucson. My mother has always loved to be on the go — any way but by air. So it was a bittersweet farewell at the airport.

For any of us, air travel is harder than it used to be; it is not as glamorous, more an ordeal. My theory is that all airports are built on land stolen from the Indians and their ghostly curse visited on us manifests itself in cancelled flights, crowded jetways, nothing but fast food restaurants and loud travelers with cell phones. The trip was necessary, however, and she was traveling with her sacred granddaughter. Still, it wasn't a festive occasion. And because airport dining is like eating at the State Fair, I packed her a little picnic basket — cold chicken sandwiches, deviled eggs, and because of my mother's sweet tooth, a dessert. With wet eyes and tiny waves, off she went.

The first trip I remember Mother sending me on was a train trip in Kansas. I went from Coffeyville to Wichita to visit my cousins. She put me on the train with a Hershey bar and a magazine to look through. The magazine didn't hold much fascination (although it seemed very grown up to have it) but the Hershey bar was a big hit.

That was about the last of the train service, so in future summers I went to Wichita on the bus. I was put in the seat directly behind the bus driver, for safety; he would keep an eye on me. A refreshment stop at a café along the way offered sandwiches cut diagonally and wrapped in waxed paper in what was called "drugstore style." It struck me as a very fancy way of serving sandwiches and I was amazed to learn that my mother knew how to do it. She taught me how to prepare sandwiches in the drugstore wrap.

She was artistic, my father was gregarious and they filled my childhood with children's parties that were the envy of my friends. One birthday party was a hayride with real horses and a hot dog roast in the country. For children's parties she made what was elegant food for small town Oklahoma in the 1950s — hors d'oeuvres of wiener, cheese and pickle on a toothpick. She taught me that parties should be fun, with food that can be simple but festive. Most of all, make sure there is lots of it with bowls and platters heaping.

My mother made me colorful, homemade costumes for Halloween. Once, I was a gypsy with great golden earrings made of the rings from canning jars. She was friendly and hospitable; my cousins and friends were always welcome.

It seemed such an ordinary family to me that I didn't realize how extraordinary it was. Barbecues in the summer featured baked beans and barbecued chicken. You knew the chicken was done when it was charred black. Fishing trips to Grand Lake included hot chocolate and popcorn at the fireplace. Summer driving vacations to New Orleans and the Gulf Coast meant mounds of fried, fresh shrimp in our cabins and pecan pralines from street merchants.

After my mother and father retired, they bought a motor home and seemed to be on the road all the time. Her idea of a great day, she said, is breakfast in Tulsa and dinner in Albuquerque. Her motto: Go see the other side of the mountain.

So many of my memories of my mother and my childhood involve food: Snow ice cream made with the second snowfall of the winter. (We had to wait for the second snow because she believed the season's first snow cleaned the air.) Fudge that you beat until you thought your arm would fall off, and when it still didn't set, fudge sauce spread on saltine crackers. Fluffy desserts that she taught me to make on Saturday mornings — angel food cakes and pies with towering meringues.

I could never match her skill at frying fish. She would roll fillets of crappie or bass in cornmeal and deep-fry them as golden and light as an Oklahoma sunset.

When I was young, my parents would have card parties that began with sausage and waffle suppers. Then they would play canasta or poker into the night. When I was in college, my friends loved to go home with me for the big country breakfasts of pork chops, bacon, pancakes and platters of fried eggs. My mother danced and laughed and made hot chili and was the mother my friends wished they had.

So with all that history of food, it seemed natural to send her off to Tucson with a picnic. It wasn't a happy trip. She was almost eighty and going to see a geriatric oncologist about treatment for cancer of the bone marrow. But it was too late. Two weeks later, she made her last trip, home from Tucson for her funeral. The driver to the cemetery remembered her wistfully. "She made the best pies of anyone I ever knew," he said.

She would want the mourners to wear bright colors and to celebrate life. And if there is not lots of food after the service, she will be very disappointed with me and my sister for being poor hostesses.

ENTERTAINING CULTURE

BURNOUT

I like to take seminars, workshops and self-help classes. Even when I don't see much self-improvement, I learn something. At the least, they are good entertainment.

In a tai chi class, one of my classmates accused me of stealing her new tennis shoes. Which, it turned out, I had done, but accidentally and I corrected it right away. Still, it upset the harmony of the class.

Then I took a seminar about panic and anxiety where the tension level was as taut as a wire. To make matters worse, after the first meeting, a woman fell down a flight of stairs and had to be rushed to the hospital with a concussion.

I attended a headache lecture where the audience was approximately 200 people, all holding their heads or leaning on one another. I suppose it was to accommodate this ailing mob that the lights were turned so low we could barely see the speakers.

When I walked into a seminar about job burnout, it reminded me of a zombie movie. I haven't seen so many people looking so blank since I was stranded overnight in O'Hare airport by rain and flood.

My assigned teammate at the burnout seminar was an employee at a zoo. "I work with large animals," he said. "I've had the same job for twenty years. I'm exhausted. Let someone else chase the gazelle when it gets loose."

Now there's a philosophy that should be stitched on a pillow.

I don't know about the rest of the class, but as soon as the seminar was over, I went right back to overworking compulsively. It was years before I changed my lifestyle. Since then I have learned a lot about chronic and cumulative stress, the snaky precursors of burnout. The health effects are more serious than feeling plum tuckered, as my Great Aunt Maude used to say. The neuroendocrine system can be damaged. Results can be migraines, heart conditions, digestive disorders, back and neck pain, skin problems, high blood pressure and clinical depression.

The underlying reasons for overwork and overstress are a web of heredity, biology, background, lifestyle and mindset. A friend in Europe attributes it to the unhealthy national work ethic and pleasure complex. "Americans have read too much Hawthorne," she said. It's a good line, but I don't know that she knows any more about stress than my friend from the zoo.

Luckily, there is a mountain of information about coping with stress. As with everything else, we have to shop around and find what works for us and then keep at it.

One book referred to this as self-healing and says visits to doctors drop thirty-four per cent by people who practice stress reduction. This involves more than unwinding in front of the TV or taking a lavender bath, although I count those as minor stress reducers.

Deep relaxation, one of the most beneficial remedies, involves meditation, abdominal breathing and progressive muscle relaxation. The goal is to decrease the heart rate, blood pressure, muscle tension and analytical thinking, which will improve health and well-being.

The purpose is not just to float around as spacey

as old hippies from the 1960s wearing tie-dyed shirts and playing with Hackensack balls. Reducing stress improves concentration and increases creativity.

One doctor/author, Edmund J. Bourne, prescribes rest, relaxation and relationships, in this dosage: at least one hour a day, one day per week, one week in every twelve to sixteen weeks.

Here are ten of the best ways to reduce stress:

1. Sleep more. Most Americans suffer from sleep deprivation.
2. Meditate, if only ten minutes a day.
3. Breathe. Take a couple of deep breaths every now and then. Learn about abdominal breathing and yoga's calm breathing.
4. Get some hobbies and new interests.
5. Exercise regularly.
6. Eat wisely, observing wholesome nutrition. And no caffeine.
7. Listen to Mozart. Classical music is calming.
8. Simplify and unclutter your environment.
9. Get therapeutic massages.
10. Play.

For best results, don't pick just one or two, but add all ten to your lifestyle.

The burnout seminar recommended taking a mini-vacation at least every six weeks, even if it meant only turning off the phone for the weekend.

My ideal way to handle stress is to adopt a holiday state of mind. On a vacation, I want to see everything, play a lot and still get lots of rest. That's how I want to live all the time. I want to think of every month as June, National Iced

Tea Month, a good time to try out this approach, to sit quietly on the porch, to think about what is important and to watch the gazelles run by.

VISIONS OF SUGARPLUMS

One recent December I was sitting in a theatre trying to add up how many performances I've seen of *The Nutcracker.* Somewhere between 250 and 300.

At the time I was doing publicity for the Kirov Ballet's *Nutcracker* tour and numbers were on my mind. There were 221 people in this production, 350 costumes, 800 hats and 450 pairs of pointe shoes and boots.

Most of my work was done and I was sitting in the theater in San Jose, California, waiting for photographers and watching the technical rehearsal, which was going very badly. There were problems with the scenery and the equipment, concern about the music, and worst of all, the rehearsal was running into overtime. People were tired and frustrated and yelling. All-in-all, it looked like a normal *Nutcracker r*ehearsal.

For fifteen years I was the manger of Tulsa Ballet Theatre which toured *Nutcracker* throughout Middle America and I know the backstage problems, obstacles and drama that lie behind those shimmering visions of sugarplums.

Every November and December it was my job to troupe forty or fifty people in trucks, buses and vans around the country giving productions of the holiday ballet in school auditoriums, civic centers, municipal theaters, Masonic halls and anywhere else somebody would pay us to perform. Nobody ever wanted us in, say, Florida. Oh, no — Oklahoma, Kansas, Nebraska, Wyoming, Texas and Arkansas, that's where our art called us. Being on tour isn't like motoring in the country. It means the curtain goes up at eight p.m.

in Lubbock or Great Bend, and if you want your check, you'll be there no matter what.

And oh the hair-raising stories I could tell you about getting there — driving with the technical crew through the night and a blizzard to get to Cheyenne, Wyoming, or the trek to Akron, Ohio, where the bus froze and we had to carpool the dancers to the theater with friends, relatives and kind strangers. On the way home, the truck carrying the scenery broke down. Then caught fire.

In Colorado, Clara threw the wooden nutcracker too hard and it sailed into the orchestra pit where it beaned a second violinist. He came back gamely to play Act II wearing a big bandage on his temple and a yellow hard hat. In a college theatre in Kansas, the fire sprinklers came on by accident and flooded the stage and scenery. In McAlester, Oklahoma, site of the state penitentiary, the volunteer stagehands turned out to be a crew of prisoners, which made me jumpy.

During *Nutcracker* season, the weather was always bad and the dancers were always sick. Buses wouldn't start, trucks froze, and crew vehicles were wrecked while we fought to stay on schedule. Lighting equipment malfunctioned and sound systems went dead. One year the stagehands kept loading too much gun powder in the canon and every time it went off it scared the little mice so badly they wet their costumes. The wardrobe personnel were furious.

One particularly awful year, when the final curtain came down on the Kingdom of the Sweets, I couldn't figure out how many people had quit. There was the stage manager, who had quit twice, once on tour and again back in the home theatre. And the principal male dancer, who had resigned in two languages, both of them angry and profane. And a wardrobe mistress, who had been so upset she cursed the little angels and ran out in tears. The photographer quit and he wasn't even an employee of ours.

So, I know about making holiday magic. It's the same with organizing the church nativity pageant or having the whole family for holiday dinner — a lot harder than it looks.

Considering all of those Ghosts of *Nutcrackers* Past, I was feeling pretty happy in San José because the current disasters were not my responsibility. When time came for a supper break, while others ranted and pounded tabletops in frustration, I went for a walk.

The night was crisp and fragrant in that lush Southern California climate, a place poetically named the Valley of the Heart's Delight. I walked by St. Joseph's cathedral just in time to see an open-air Christmas pageant in the courtyard. It was an original musical production of *Las Posadas*, the popular Hispanic story of Mary and Joseph's search for lodging. The church's music director had written it and was conducting a little orchestra with great vigor.

This was an upbeat version. The angel who appears to the shepherds was a local gospel singer wearing a funky Bo Peep costume. Until then, the sheep had been content to follow one another around the plywood mountains singing "Bah bah bah." But once they heard the Good News, they were transformed. They pushed away the cutout scenery and used their sheeplike talent to become a troupe of tap dancers. They were teenagers in high-topped tennis shoes with taps and lots of energy.

Just before the finale, a character in the play stepped forward — I think it was the donkey — and said that although admission was free, this performance was a fund raiser for the church's street ministry to help all of those who, like Mary and Joseph, had no place to sleep that night. What an appeal. We all *ran* to the donation box.

The next night, the Kirov's professional production of *The Nutcracker* opened with the precision of a polished diamond. Across town, a plump angel belted out her message and behold — the whole valley seemed to dance.

MUSIC NOTES

My hair, lately, is so bad I look like Hector Berlioz.

I know that because I've been reading *The Lives of the Great Composers* and I saw a picture of him.

I have always liked to read about art and artists, sort of elbowing my way into the crowd. I started with biographical works of novelists. Then playwrights. Then poets with their lives of boiling passions. Now I have discovered musicians.

I've developed a special fondness for music program notes. Balanchine said program notes should be "an invitation to the dance," but the programs that really sizzle are those for classical music. Those writers mix words together like an intoxicating drink — ice and fire and shimmering colors.

The program notes for a Tulsa Concertime performance of Mozart's *Viola Quintet in G Minor* were written by Melvin Berger. He described the "sorrowful character" of this quintet with its "broken sighs and gasps," the "prevailing melancholy" of the third movement and the "slow pulsing chords in the inner voices" of the fourth movement.

In Beethoven's *String Quartet in D Major*, Berger says that the "bombast plays itself out" and that the movement ends with a "whispered farewell."

That's hot stuff. It's much more than an invitation to the music; it grabs you right out of the audience for a sultry tango.

I have a theory about this cult of celebrity we live in.

I think part of it is propelled by a universal feeling of being insignificant and helpless. We yearn for heroes.

Many celebrities are glorified, but anything but heroes. The biographical figures of history used to be portrayed one-dimensionally, pure and noble. Their lives didn't read anything at all like the Greek gods who leap off the page lustful, vengeful and red-toothed just like the folks we know. In the opposite extreme, the influence of tabloid journalism produces biographies that pant with a steamy recitation of scandals, armchair psychological analysis and tawdry behavior. This prompted some wag to say, "Biography has given death a new terror."

I appreciate the modern trend toward biographical balance. I like to know that Einstein was a bad father and a neglectful husband, a genius but human. Otherwise, it encourages us all to be sanctimonious and judgmental, about other people, of course.

That's why I like the stories of the lives of great composers. They are full personalities: Satie walked a pet lobster on a leash; Brahms was handsome but cynical and bad tempered; Schubert was only 5'1", and so plump he was nicknamed Tubby; Handel had his rages and such a dry wit that a contemporary said he behaved "as if he could not count to five;" Tchaikovsky was so neurotic he thought that while he was conducting his head would fall off and roll across the floor; Liszt was a magnetic ladies' man. A colleague called him "Mephistopheles in a cassock." When Liszt performed, women swooned and fought over the gloves he tossed to the stage floor.

One of my favorite music stories — perhaps as much myth as fact — involves a composer and a choreographer, Stravinsky and Nijinsky. It was the opening night in Paris of the ballet *The Rite of Spring*. When the audience heard the discordant music, the theatre erupted in bedlam. The clamor from the audience was so loud that the dancers couldn't hear the beats, so Nijinsky stood in the wings shouting counts at them. Half of the audience was on its feet cheering and the other half was booing. Stravinsky blew his top and stopped conducting long enough to yell back at the audience, "Go to hell!"

Now that's a night at the theatre. Wouldn't you have loved to go out for a drink with these two artists afterwards and listen to them fume and rage, and then start planning their next work.

FIVE-STAR BOOKSTORES

This summer, when everyone else is traveling frantically and complaining about how awful it is, what I want to do is browse in peaceful bookstores.

Many summers ago, I went on vacation to a South Carolina beach with a new black bathing suit and the best selling novel *Jaws*. I put a low beach chair on the white sand and a tall, iced drink beside it. With the warm ocean lapping at my feet, I began to read about a shark's terrorizing a resort area. Ever so often I stopped reading just long enough to pull my chair away from the water. Soon I was sitting up in the sea grass. I didn't go into the water that entire vacation. I wouldn't go on the water in a boat. I wouldn't even walk very *near* the ocean. That experience taught me to be more prudent about my summer reading materials and about my leisure time.

I enjoy light reading, but I don't take reading lightly. I remember calling a friend who was dying with lung cancer.

"What are you doing today?" I asked.

"Reading," she said.

"What are you reading?"

"You know those books we're all going to read some day? Well, I'm reading them."

Conversations like that remind me to be mindful. Some special memories are of great bookstores I have visited.

I think about the multi-level Tattered Cover book store in Denver with its cozy chairs for reading, the mugs of latté in the basement of Elliot Bay Books on Seattle's waterfront, the creepy spiral staircase of the Mysterious Bookshop in New York and the rain on the conservatory roof of Kramerbooks in Washington D.C.'s Dupont Circle.

No matter where I travel, I come home lugging heavy bags of books. They are my favorite travel keepsakes. The bookstore and the books I discovered there are twin memories. In the rambling Chinook Bookshop in Colorado Springs, Colorado, I first found May Sarton's journals; those journals taught me to appreciate solitude. In the Book Warehouse in Victoria, British Columbia, I found an illustrated salmon cookbook that changed my diet if not my life. In a smart little bookstore in Beaufort, South Carolina, I found Norman Maclean's riveting and elegant *Young Men and Fire.*

Tulsa is a city rich with bookstores. I frequent most of them. I'm particularly fond of the old drugstore atmosphere of Steve's Sundries with its good inventory of books and magazines and a counter where you can get a grilled cheese sandwich and a cherry Coke. Novel Idea, by contrast, is upscale, both in cuisine and inventory. Borders' comfortable coffee shop, quiet by day, often features musical entertainment at night. Scribner's is elegant, and Barnes and Noble is expansive. The Happy Griffin is an independent bookstore with a witty décor. Oak Tree Books is one of the most orderly shops for used and rare books. These are just a sampling.

It takes more than an extensive inventory to make a great bookstore. Memorable bookstores have character and atmosphere, but they don't have the hushed respect of fine libraries, a different love. Five-star bookstores embrace the books with a genuineness that cannot be faked, and they hold a special welcome for readers. Readers know a great bookstore at once. The moment we step inside, we sense it and sigh, feeling at home and at rest.

It's no surprise that bookstores have become the community watering holes of the Information Age. Bookstores are being called havens for the intellect, sanctuaries of civility and cultural anchors in the fragmented world. An article in *USA Today* said that bookstores are one of the last public places where people feel safe and mentally enriched.

Bookstores with coffee shops are oases of unhurried time where people have business meetings, sit alone and scribble in journals, do homework, peck at laptop computers and gather for discussions and lectures. Bookstores seem to fill a hunger for community. Socialization and privacy mingle there. To me, they are what Hemingway meant by a clean, well-lighted place.

As wonderful as that seems, the book industry issued a grim report in the spring of 1999; book sales had dropped for the first time since 1990. Although more books are available — from independent booksellers, grocery stores, drugstores, mega bookstores and on-line — book sales are down three per cent. Americans bought thirty million fewer books than the previous year.

Once upon a time, paperback books, inexpensive and portable, ushered in a revolution in popular reading. For the first time, the paperback book sales have fallen. The sharpest decline in sales, twenty percent, was among the 18-25 age group. Young people are not buying books. They're too busy and too mobile; buying books is not a priority for their discretionary dollars. But we cannot lay all of the blame among the twentysomethings; there was a ten percent sales drop among people ages 40-49.

The great food writer, M.F.K. Fisher, was often asked why she wrote about food and not about bigger issues, such as power and love. She replied that she thought the three basic needs — food, security and love — are so entwined, she could not think about one without the others. For her, rice in the bowl evoked nourishment in the heart.

It is the same with reading, is it not? I can never think of Fitzgerald without remembering the first time I read *Tender is the Night* one summer in a small Oklahoma town, sunbathing in the front yard, but reading about troubled ladies with pearls in the south of France, reading and waiting for college, reading and longing for escape from childhood, confinement and a small town.

So while I'm remembering books and bookstores that have changed my life, I'm going to hope that people begin buying books again before bookstores become yet another endangered place on the planet. I'm going to hope that young people discover the exotic worlds of books. And I'm going to hope that people begin reading books before reading books becomes a quaint but extinct practice of a lost civilization.

FENG SHUI

I'd rather not go into why, but I called in a feng shui consultant the other day. Feng shui is the ancient Chinese art of placement. It's based on the belief that our life and destiny are influenced by the chi, or energy, of the universe and nature.

Feng shui is trendy in interior decorating. There are feng shui kits and accessories in catalogs and a whole shelf of feng shui books at the nearest bookstore. And, for those of us who don't want to do it ourselves, there are feng shui consultants.

My consultants happened to be two women and a fuzzy dog in a van from Arkansas.

The fuzzy dog stayed in the van, but the two women came in carrying gadgets and ready to balance my energy. One had some kind of meter that measured the electromagnetic field in my house. The reading was alarmingly high which could explain why I am, to use their phrase, sick and weakly. The other one carried two metal things like water dowsers that spun in her hands.

They came in making suggestions about rearranging the furniture, which is what they were supposed to do and what I had invited them to do, but it threw me into some weird personality shift. I took their comments as an attack on my creative decorating genius and immediately became the Client from Hell.

When they came across a bank of dried roses in the dining room, one of them shook her head and said, "Mm, Mm, Mm — all this *dryness*. Tell me, have you had challenges with money?"

I bristled. Did she have any idea how hard it was to dry those roses and arrange them like that? Doesn't she know how fashionable this is? Doesn't she read *Victoria* magazine?

So, I began to lie to the consultants.

"Challenges with money?" I repeated, as if it were an idea so alien to me that I could barely grasp it. "Not particularly."

She suggested living plants instead, something green, but I had my arms crossed obstinately and wouldn't answer. The dining room is much too dark for a live plant to survive here; anyone could see that.

We moved to the bedroom. She pointed to one corner.

"That's where you should have your bed. You'll rest better if you face the door."

"I don't want my bed there," I said petulantly. '"I want to face the east. I want to look out on the garden."

"But that's the most powerful spot in the room," she insisted. "Besides, it's the key to your relationships. Tell me, have you had challenges with relationships?"

If I'd had an honest bone in my body, I would have laughed at the question until I had to lean against the wall for support. I would have laughed until tears streamed down my face and flooded the bedroom, the powerful relationship corner and everything else.

But I wasn't honest. What I said with a straight face was, "Who me?'"

I did take another, reluctant look at that relationship hot spot and here's what I saw: a chest of drawers with one broken leg, full of clothes I can't wear anymore, and on the chest — an antique hat that belonged to my late grandmother and an urn with the ashes of my dead cat. If these articles symbolize "relationship" in my life, I'm just a tick away from a sèance and talking to a Ouiji Board.

Maybe the feng shui ladies are on to something, I thought. I felt my resistance and bad temper begin to melt. I was paying for it, I reasoned; I may as well give it a try.

Overall, the consultants' basic advice was to have more open space so the chi can move easily, and to have most of the furniture facing the doors. This welcomes opportunity, they said. Well, who couldn't use more of that.

As soon as they left, I flew into action. I began hauling some of the furniture out to the garage and shoving the rest of it around, and that led to rigorous cleaning. They had installed some magnets to redirect those electromagnetic currents, and as eerie as it sounds, the minute they did that I felt — I don't know — lighter.

I hung wind chimes over the front door, swept the leaves off the porch and got a cheery doormat. They recommended red. I got green, thinking, "I can't be a slave to advice;" besides, I couldn't find red. The point of sprucing up the front door area, they had told me, is to invite in knowledge and good luck. For good measure, I did the same thing at the back door.

"Pleeese come in, Chi," I said.

In the bedroom, I did something about the biting doors, doors which bang into one another, because resolving that architectural problem will help me resolve or avoid conflict in my life. I moved the bed to the place the broken chest had been. I even moved the cat's ashes to another room.

"What the hey," I said aloud, madcap with abandon; "let's give relationships a little boost." They had suggested I install something symbolizing relationships in that spot, so I hung a birdhouse from a rustic clothes tree. Nesting or free as a bird — Chi, take your pick, I thought.

With apologies to *Victoria*, I took down the dried roses and moved a huge, trailing ivy into the dining room. And you know what? It's doing fine there. I have to admit it, the live plant makes the space seem, well, livelier.

In the kitchen, in the corner symbolizing wealth, I set a plump, green piggy bank.

The concept of feng shui is to live in harmony with energy and the environment; the goal is to maximize health, wealth and happiness. I don't believe it's foolproof. I mean, look at all the trouble the Hong Kong stock market has had and don't you know they are knee deep in feng shui consultants?

It could have been the aerobic exercise of housecleaning, or the psychological lift a clean, rearranged house brings, or the restful atmosphere of a minimalist dècor, but, whatever the reason, I am sleeping better. I feel more energized or, I guess you could say, not so weak and sickly. Plus, I got an unexpected refund check from my insurance company, so maybe the wealth corner is beginning to kick in. The check is for only $26, but you've got to start somewhere.

Except for the magnets, the feng shui consultants didn't try to sell me stuff or recommend expensive redecorating.

"What we find," they said, "is that people usually have everything they need. It's just in the wrong place."

That, I believe, is profound wisdom. So maybe the chi is moving briskly around the house and splashing a little knowledge on me as it passes by.

AMERICAN LIBRARY IN PARIS

One of the best things about travelling is seeing things with new eyes, not just where you are, but where you've been all this time.

On a trip to France, I visited the American Library in Paris. To my eyes, it was an ordinary library, but one with a romantic history and a surprising impact.

During World War I, the American Library Association sent thousands of books and magazines to American troops to keep up the morale of the homesick doughboys. When the Great War ended, it seemed the wartime library would disappear, but a campaign to save it sprang up. *The New York Herald* launched a campaign to save the library as a monument to America.

The first donation was made by the father of Alan Seegar, the fallen soldier and poet who wrote, "I Have a Rendezvous with Death."

The library was saved and it introduced new concepts to Europeans, such as the Dewey decimal system and public access to books. And not only did it survive, it endured tumultuous times — the Depression of the 1930s, World War II and the Nazi Occupation. It became an emotional and intellectual refuge. For English-speaking residents, the American Library in Paris was a home away from home. It was a gathering place for some of the most influential American and British writers of the twentieth century: Ernest Hemingway, James Joyce, Ford Maddox Ford and Thorton Wilder worked there. Stephen Vincent Benet wrote "John Brown's Body" there.

Edith Wharton sat on the board of trustees; Gertrude Stein visited often. Patrons and donors are a Who's Who list of literature and arts: Julia Child, Olivia de Havilland, Henry Miller and Ford Maddox Ford. Special collections were donated by Marlene Dietrich, Sylvia Beach and Janet Flanner.

In the 1920s, the library published its own magazine, the *Ex Libris*, which included book reviews and recommended reading lists. In the 1930s, it began a series called *Evenings with an Author* which continues to this day and has featured writers from Colette to Betty Friedan.

During World War II, the library again hoisted its mandate to serve servicemen and women in battle and sent publications to the front lines and, when possible, to prison camps.

Even during the Occupation, the library kept its doors open, committed to maintaining morale to the best of its ability. It was a place to meet for those doing charity work, share news of home and talk about the prevailing situation. When a Nazi order forbade Jewish members from entering the library, books were delivered secretly to those members at home.

Today the American Library in Paris, located in the shadow of the Eiffel Tower, is the largest English-language library in continental Europe with 90,000 volumes, primarily works by American and English-language authors. Like nonprofit organizations everywhere, it is struggling for financial donations.

When William Styron was the guest speaker there, he spoke eloquently about his passion for libraries. When he was seventeen, Mr. Styron said, "the United States Marine Corps introduced me to the glories of the library. The library became my hangout, my private club, my sanctuary, the place of my salvation ... When I was reading in the library, I was sheltered from the world and from the evil winds of the future; no harm could come to me there. It also brought me immeasurable enrichment.'

Back home in Tulsa, when I visit my own neighborhood branch library, I see it with a new reverence. I hope I always will.

ADVICE FROM MY FRIENDS

What's the word for being able to hold two opposing opinions at the same time? I mean, completely contradictory positions. You know, like Congress, on the one hand arguing that NEA funding should be cut because it might fund obscene material and at the same spending $40 million to produce the best selling pornographic book in American history — the Starr Report.

Well, whatever it's called — dichotomy or paradox — that describes how I feel about the counsel I've been getting from my friends.

I love my friends and I remember the adage: *God gives us our relatives; thank God we can choose our friends.* What I'm talking about is advice from my friends. I'm lucky to have vocal, self-confident friends who aren't afraid to speak their minds. In the past, they have given me advice that has saved, if not my life, at least my sanity.

When I was getting ready to make a long flight to France, one friend said, "Trust me on this. On the plane, wear pants with an elastic waistband." And another said, "You'll have to carry your luggage through customs. Believe me, you have to have a suitcase with wheels." These two pieces of advice were so good and sound, I went around singing, "I really do get by with a little help from my friends."

Then, just as I was coasting along thinking how lucky I am to have fallen in with such a wise bunch, something catastrophic went wrong with my car and I couldn't decide what to do about it. Nothing brings out advice like the subject of cars.

The other top contenders are jobs and hair.

"What do you think I ought to do with my hair — perm, cut, color?" This is a question you can ask of total strangers and launch an in-depth discussion.

Friends also have lots of opinions about careers and professional interactions and are happy to give it, such as, "Just march in and tell him ..."

And we all have lots of advice about one another's mates and dates and ex's. It's funny, but we're not asked for this as often as we once were.

My car's transmission was another story. Everybody had a position and defended it like the Alamo. "*Absolutely* keep the car and fix it," some said. "*Definitely* get rid of the car and get a new one," others said. "Buy, lease, new, used, repair" — advice bombarded me. Overnight, my friends were in two camps — repair or purchase — and each was armed to the teeth with facts. They would call and begin conversations with, "I checked with my mechanic and he said ..." or "I looked it up in the Blue Book and ..."

A competitive edge crept into their voices. "Have you made a decision yet?" they would ask, and the question was ominous and heavy, as if they were implying, "My friendship and my advice are bound together. Take both or lose both forever — and I just hope you're prepared to live with your choice." I stopped talking about my car problem with anybody. I made the decision myself in the dark of night, with the lights off and the shades pulled.

The experience reminded me of all the bad advice I've received over the years. Advice such as: "You don't need a computer *class*; the best thing to do is just figure it out yourself." Or, "You won't need a reservation this time of year." And award-winning bad advice such as, "What you ought to do is get back with your ex," or "You're not too old to adopt a child," or "Move out of town and start all over." The whopper of bad advice came in my teens and should have taught me once and for all about the fallibility of friendly advice. "Oh, don't get contact lenses," someone told me, "you look good in glasses." Which leads me to conclude that advice is usually not black or white. It's black and white. When Diogenes was asked, "What's difficult?" he replied, "To know oneself." And when he was asked, "What's easy?" he said, "To advise another."

I have learned that my wise, beloved, opinionated friends can be as ignorant and misguided as I am, and that it's up to me to sift through the advice and separate the wheat from the... oh, I get it. It's like commercials or politicians.

PRIMA BALLERINA ASSOLUTA

It is rare to be able to describe someone as a "legend" and to know that the word is justified. In the world of ballet, a genuine legend was Alexandra Danilova who died July 13, 1997.

She was *prima ballerina assoluta* — the highest honorary title awarded by critics and audiences.

Her career began with the Imperial Russian Ballet of St. Petersburg, now known as the Kirov Ballet. She was most famous in the 1930s and 1940s, touring the world with the Ballet Russe de Monte Carlo. That ballet company crisscrossed the United States, introducing a whole nation to ballet. It was the first company to travel by bus. Sometimes the dancers stopped to take company class by the side of the road, holding on to the barbed wire as a ballet barre while astonished cattle looked on.

Danilova's most celebrated roles were in *Gaité Parisienne, Le Beau Danube, Coppelia and La Sonambula.* She was known for her champagne sparkle, her luminous charisma on stage and "the most beautiful legs in ballet." After she retired from dancing, she was a teacher at the School of American Ballet in New York, which had been founded by her lifetime friend and former lover George Balanchine.

I never saw her perform, but I worked with her during my years as a ballet company manager. She was in Tulsa several times and we had dinners at the Russian Tea Room in New York. Even off-stage, she was always a great ballerina and very glamorous. She took the role seriously. She introduced me to the concept of an "everyday fur," as opposed to one's better fur coats for special occasions.

Once, at a big ballet reception in New York, in a room so crowded with guests and press that you could hardly move, or breathe, somebody got Danilova a chair. She was the only one in the room sitting. I watched as, one by one, the New York press and ballet luminaries made their way to her to pay her homage and literally kneel at her feet.

Her friends called her Choura, the Russian diminutive for Alexandra, like Maggie for Margaret in English. I asked her once about making the movie *The Turning Point* with Shirley MacLaine, Anne Bancroft and Mikhail Baryshnikov. I gathered everybody was being very Hollywood and calling her Choura. Baryshnikov was at the apex of his career.

"How did he behave toward you?" I asked.

"Very polite," she said, "very respectful. He sat with me and talked quietly."

"And what did he call you?"

She looked surprised, as if there was only one way that a well-mannered young Soviet artist could behave. "He called me," she said, "Madame." I have always liked Baryshnikov for that.

I am told that she could be very imperial, much the ballerina, but I never saw that. In one of Agnes de Mille's autobiographical books, Miss de Mille, who could be pretty imperial herself, wrote about creating the American ballet *Rodeo* for the Ballet Russe in 1942. It was a nightmare. The Russian dancers hated her and the ballet and de Mille hated them back. On opening night, de Mille was to dance the role of the Cowgirl; she was so nervous, she was throwing up. Danilova, who was not in *Rodeo*, went to her dressing room and did up de Mille's hair so it wouldn't come loose when she danced. For the premiere of *Rodeo*, de Mille reported with abiding gratitude, the great Alexandra Danilova was her maid.

I remember a small dinner party that showed the glitter of Danilova's charm. She liked a couple of drinks before dinner, white wine perhaps, and then to linger over dinner and tell funny stories. She told one story herself. Dance companies are often a melting pot of nationalities and this was the point of a story Danilova told about being introduced to a child of dancers.

"I said to him in Russian, 'Do you speak Russian?' No answer. So I said to him in French, 'Do you speak French?' No answer. So I said to him in English, 'Do you speak English?' Still no answer. 'What language does this child speak?' I asked the parents. 'None, Madame Danilova,' they said. 'He's only two.'" And then she laughed and laughed at that story on herself.

"There's a Russian proverb," she wrote, "*You make your own happiness.*" I believe it.

She herself had no children, no family at all when she died at age ninety-three. She said that she had sacrificed country, marriage and children — everything — to be a ballerina. But, she wrote, "There was never any misunderstanding on my part. I knew the price. I put my dancing first, before my allegiances to friends and lovers, even husbands, before my home. I gave 100 per cent of myself to my art and my art has repaid me." But life as a dancer in the Ballet Russe was not without passion, intrigue, feuds, petit scandals, even a murder.

At a reunion of Ballet Russe dancers in New York, a television reporter preparing a documentary asked Madame Danilova about the early days with that company and if there had been any romances. Among the former dancers in that room alone was a tangled history of marriage, divorce, affairs, trysts and alliances. Danilova did not reply. She sat regally in silence, then she began to laugh quietly and she laughed until tears came to her eyes and her false eyelashes became unglued. They had to stop the cameras to let her collect herself. She murmured something in Russian under her breath to a friend.

"What did she say?" I asked later.

"She said, 'What a question!'"

One of the times she was in Tulsa, we arranged for Saks to have an autograph session of her memoirs, the book titled *Choura*. The event was a great success and she was enormously pleased. It is a lovely book, spare and elegant, not sentimental but with whiffs of poetry that take away your breath.

Danilova was born in St. Petersburg in 1903, orphaned at an early age, taken in by her babushka (grandmother), who died, and then by an adopted aunt, who also died. All of this before the age of seven. "My refuge," she said, "was my imagination." Then it was discovered that she had a talent for dancing and at the age of eight she entered the famous Maryinsky School and began her way to becoming a ballerina.

She was in St. Petersburg when the Russian Revolution began in 1917; in her memoirs, she calls it "some trouble in the streets." Through her book passes an extraordinary cast of characters from her life: Serge Diaghilev,

Coco Chanel, Leonide Massine, Michel Fokine, the famous Baby Ballerinas, Igor Stravinsky, Pablo Picasso and her long-time dance partner Frederic Franklin. She recalled the time she accidentally knocked out one of Freddie's teeth while practicing her pirouettes. "What a drama," she recalled wryly.

The predominant figure is Balanchine, a friend from childhood. They lived together as husband and wife for seven years. In Monte Carlo, he played Bach on the piano far into the night and gambled at the casino to win enough money to pay their hotel bills. She writes of the ballets he created for her, ballets that turned the pages of history. The choreography, she said, just poured out of him. *Mozartiana,* she writes, "was pearls of pure dancing, a long strand of beautiful steps strung together by the music." His ballet *Serenade* was "like a wave," a ballet set in moonlight under "a moon so cold and disturbing, a little bit treacherous and very mystical."

My favorite Danilova story is from *Choura*, about her final performance in 1957. "In Russia," she wrote, "we were taught never to touch our knees to the floor when taking a bow unless there was royalty. We were to go on our knees only to royalty or to God." Her farewell performance was flooded with flowers, confetti and tears. When she took her final curtain call, she said, "I spread the flowers I had been sent at my feet and as a gesture of thanks for the support and devotion I had received over the course of my career, I went down on my knee to my audience."

Choura, The Memoirs of Alexandra Danilova,
Alfred A. Knopf, 1986

WOMEN'S LIB – GO GIRL!

I watched the two-part television documentary by Ken Burns about Susan B. Anthony and Elizabeth Cady Stanton, and although I knew the skeleton of the story of their reform work, I was left meek and humbled by their heroism. For almost sixty years they championed rights for women: the right for women to go to college, hold a job, own property, work outside the home in professions, have custody of their children and — the special crusade of Anthony and Stanton — the right to vote. These are heritages I take for granted, like an ungrateful daughter of privilege. Yet against incredible odds, Anthony and Stanton worked for these rights their whole lives. They died before they could cast a ballot themselves, but today that reform movement is called "the largest social transformation in American history." It was the pattern for the civil rights movement.

I was not around for that pioneer suffragette work. Suffrage — from the Latin word meaning, "to vote for" and with the Biblical definition "a short intercessory prayer or petition." The suffragettes campaigned and petitioned from the 1840s until 1920 when thirty-six states ratified the amendment to the U.S. Constitution to grant women the right to vote. Oklahoma was one of those thirty-six states; two states trailed in later, but ten of the forty-eight states still did not approve the radical notion of women's voting in elections.

I was around for another wave of feminist activity, the decade of the 1970s. I was a young woman just starting my career. It was the heyday of the women's lib movement when much of our focus — and certainly my self-serving interest — was on equal work opportunities and equal pay. Ironically, I've never worn shorter skirts in my life than the 1970s when I was agitating to be taken seriously on the work front.

I look back on some of those events and am amazed at the gall, and sometimes the silliness, of our struggle. I remember being interviewed for a job as editor of an internal publication of a large Tulsa business. The previous editor had been a man, but now they specifically requested a woman. I listened to the job description.

"You have increased the workload so much, it's two jobs rolled into one," I observed, "and why do you particularly want a woman?" And the man answered, without guilt or guile, "Because we've found that women work harder and stay longer and quite frankly, we don't have to pay a woman as much." Can you imagine an employer saying that today, although in far too many cases, women still are paid less than men are for the same work.

During much of the time women's lib was at its crest, I was working at a university, which was no more enlightened than the rest of the workplace. The student body often chose reformers as guest speakers: sociologist Rollo May, consumer advocate Ralph Nader, Mary Calderone from SIECUS, the Sex Information and Education Council of the United States. Her work was controversial but highly praised. One national magazine wrote: "What Margaret Sanger did for birth control, and Rachel Carson did for the environment, Calderone has done for sex education. Her work, like theirs, has profoundly changed the quality of life in this century." She was the first person to identify me as a feminist and I blushed with pride.

Many of the guests, such as representatives from the group Bread and Roses, spoke on the explosive subject of women's lib and equal rights. The Great Hall was packed on one of these occasions and the questions from the audience were feverish as people struggled to clarify and ridicule feminism, sexism, women's lib and the odious term, "male chauvinist pig".

"Do you mean, if I open a door for a lady" one man asked, "I've discriminated against her?" At this point the speaker lost patience with the stream of nitpicky questions.

"Listen," she said. "I don't have to explain discrimination to women. A woman understands her own discrimination." And we did.

We women employees on campus had consciousness raising sessions and women's unity meetings, but perhaps the lowest moment was having to petition the administration to be allowed to wear pant suits to work. The question went all the way to the president's office and finally the edict came down; we could wear pant suits to work — one day a week.

As a young instructor and administrator, I was right in the thick of this. I have always given speeches and book reviews to organizations and civic groups. In those days I was invited to speak about women in higher education and the subject of feminism. The titillating title of that talk was, "From Adam's Rib to Women's Lib." By today's standards, it was tame stuff.

My female colleagues in the journalism department and I organized seminars especially for the women students to coach them in preparing their resumes and portfolios. We invited Carolyn Bird to campus, the author of such books as *Born Female: the High Cost of Keeping Women Down* and *Everything a Woman Needs to Know to Get Paid What She's Worth*. We held a special meeting for female students to meet with her and talk about equal pay. Only two students showed up. My colleague Susan was furious and the next day asked her protègè why she hadn't attended this valuable session to prepare her for the workforce and job hunting.

"I couldn't come," the girl said, "I had to bake brownies for my sorority."

America was born of revolution, and civil disobedience is part of our national character. But, oh, Miss Anthony, and oh, Mrs. Stanton, I think we need some of your grit.

GUILTY PLEASURES

I can't believe I watched all four hours of the Academy Awards. Even if I was ironing, or rebuilding the carburetor from my car, the awful truth is that I spent four hours gawking at celebrities. Especially awful since my favorite movie didn't win best picture and I hated Gwyneth Paltrow's dress.

It just shows me the insidiousness of this cultural obsession with celebrity and fame. It's everywhere. I read in the local newspaper that Charlie Sheen was changing his name to Charles. This breaking news was issued by his agent, who also changed Ricky Shroeder's name to Rick. I can't believe someone sent this out as a news release. I can't believe that newspapers printed it and that I read it.

Take the thorny issue of *People* magazine. Refusing to buy it seems so noble. I can't remember the last time I purchased a *People* magazine. December, I think. But only because there was a great holiday recipe for sweet potatoes. Also, the story about Kate Moss was too long to read at the checkout counter.

But does that high moral road also apply to the dentist's office? Can I read it there? And what about the slicker celebrity magazines, like *Biography and Interview*?

And what about books? I draw the line at the Lewinsky book, won't buy it, won't borrow it, wouldn't read it if I found it in the gutter. And yet, I confess, just last week I was staying awake nights to finish the dual biography of Bobby Daren and Sandra Dee, which turned out to be so depressing. I was driven to it, I believe, by a special on

OETA. I hope I've learned once and for all not to let television be my true north of taste and judgment.

I have a crackpot theory that our fascination with celebrity is because we seem to know these people better than we know our friends and neighbors. I am shocked and feel betrayed when I discover that people who have been my friends for twenty years had an abortion, or are adopted, or had a long childhood illness and I didn't know about it. In this age of public confession, celebrities would tell us this personal stuff at the drop of a hat. And they'll bring their own hat.

It is interesting to see the changes in the biography genre over the years. For a book review I gave at the Central Library's *Books Sandwiched In,* I read a hefty 500+ page biography of Rudolph Nureyev. It is a clear example of the style of biography currently popular — laboriously researched with details stacked on the page as solidly as bricks. Biographies today are more honest, yet too many go overboard. They don't just tell the life, warts and all; they tell all the warts they can find.

It was true of the Nureyev book. The research about his childhood in Russia was thorough and painstaking: born on a Trans-Siberian train, grew up in a one-room mud hut in the town of Ufa, which was nicknamed the Devil's Inkpot because it was so muddy and dark, the son of poor Tartar Muslims descended from Genghis Khan. His father was a professional soldier who beat Nureyev whenever he caught him going to dance class. As a boy, Nureyev was frail, sensitive, blond, shabby and unpolished. From childhood he had a fierce driven self-determination to dance. "All my life," he said, "even as a boy in

Russia, I had to grab life by the throat." That background is important for understanding the artist and adult he became.

Later revelations went off the rails, I thought, and the book included excessive detail about his homosexuality. Did I really want to know about his promiscuous cruising, casual sex, callboys who interrupted dinner parties, the flirtation with Mick Jagger? Actually, I did, but I shouldn't have. We want to tell the author, "Use some judgment here. You don't have to give us every grubby fact you unearthed."

Reminds me of a Harry Truman story about the time he was stumping for office and only one farmer showed up to hear his speech. "What do you want me to do?" Truman asked.

"Well," the farmer said, "if I went out to feed my cattle and only one showed up, I believe I'd feed it." So Truman gave the speech and then said, "What did you think?"

"Well," the farmer said, "if I went to feed my cattle and only one showed up, I believe I'd feed it, but I don't believe I'd feed it the whole damn load."

As a journalist, I know that people are news. As a writer, I particularly like to write profiles about people. I love to read biographies. I like to find out where people came from, how they got to be what they are, and how they are different from what we think they are.

And yet.

And yet, I am disgusted with this mania for celebrities, especially media celebrities. "Circus people" is what Alfie Woodard calls movie actors, and I like the bluntness of that.

One writer said that we have become a nation of voyeurs. If we were to judge by the magnitude of the press coverage, one of the greatest national tragedies of modern times was the death of Sonny Bono.

If you watch as much *Biography* on A & E cable as I do, you know how misplaced a lot of celebrity admiration is. Is famous and pretty everything? Doesn't education figure at all into the equation?

Melanie Griffith certainly values education. She was quoted as saying, "I wish in a way, that I had, you know, gone to college and gotten a degree. I would have tried to have gotten a degree in probably philosophy. If there is such a thing. Is there?"

I rest my case.

And so this brings me to the confession of guilty pleasures. One of my favorite indulgences is celebrity biography, although mercifully, I am growing out of it.

I have shelves of biographies of the queens of England and biographies of writers (such as Ernest Hemingway, Dorothy Parker, James Thurber, Isak Dinesen, Jane Austen) but I used to have a whole library of actors' biographies and autobiographies. David Niven's was particularly witty. One of the worst, and that means best, was written by Marlon Brando's ex-wife who got even when she got a publisher. She wrote a book titled *Brando for Breakfast* and told us that Brando is so crazy he once chewed a mouthful of bees.

Last year I read, and I mean devoured in midnight sessions, Mia Farrow's autobiography. That's a book that will turn you against Woody Allen forever, or at the very least, have you watch his movies with a new interpretation bordering on revulsion. But the companion thought to "Oh, poor Mia" is "What were you *thinking*?"

This summer's guilty pleasure was a memoir by Isabella Rossellini titled *Some of Me.* My defense, and I know it's weak, is that I got it from the library. She dropped out of school at fifteen and became, this is a quote from her book, "one of the most beautiful women in the world." Her twin sister got a Ph.D. in medieval literature and we've never heard of her. Isabella Rossellini writes about makeup, clothes, adopting animals from the SPCA, what she knows about insects, what it's like to be an international model and the best way to wash dishes; that her father, Roberto Rossellini, thought the "morally correct" camera placement was eye level; that her mother, Ingrid Bergman, was denounced from the floor of the U.S. Senate in the late 1940s for her love affair with the married film director; and about growing up in postwar Italy where she was considered rich because she and her siblings had shoes. She talks about her own husbands and lovers (Martin Scorsese, David Lynch and Gary Oldman) but not a lot, not nearly as much as Marlon Brando's ex-wife did.

I don't know why I like books like this. I tried out some puffed up theories about its being part of the human condition to search for heroes, even flawed ones like the Greek and Roman gods. Perhaps biographies are a way to try on different emotions and to measure our life against someone else's. I think really I like them because it's just jaw-dropping fun to rummage around in someone else's life. Once, on a plane over Texas, the woman next to me was absorbed in a political biography. She looked up only one time during the flight and her eyes were as round as pie pans when she said to me, "I must have been raised with my head in a bucket, because I had no idea people behaved like this."

MARKETING MOZART

There's a lot of talk about supplements and vitamins and herbs lately, but I think I've stumbled onto the real elixir of life: Mozart.

I read about some research which showed that listening to Mozart helped students increase their test scores. So, a sucker for any quick fix, I rushed to my neighborhood mega bookstore to see what I could find.

What I found was that the merchandisers had been there ahead of me. Way ahead of me. In addition to the miles of Mozart CDs, there was a special section of Mozart packaged and marketed for its psychological benefits. Self-help Wolfgang. There must have been at least twenty different CDs.

The jacket copy on the CDs quoted experts and a varied lot they were — an audiologist, a book author also known as "the dean of sound healers," an ethnomusicologist/radio personality, something vaguely referred to only as "studies" as in "studies show . . ." and "research among students at UC/Irvine." That could be anything.

After these experts and scholars had analyzed Mozart, the advertising copywriters got to work on him. Mozart was, one wrote, "the Mick Jagger of his day." Oh, I think not.

What his music will do for us today is miraculous, they say. Here are some of the claims. Listening to Mozart will:

- stir the heart and lift the test score
- raise your IQ
- increase your brain power

- manage daily stress
- promote deep relaxation, sweet dreams and power naps
- heal the body, mind and soul
- improve problem-solving skills
- enhance creativity by activating the right brain,
- reduce stress and tension by moderating heart beat, blood pressure and body temperature.

But it didn't end with merely Advertising Amadeus. Now it was time to Package Wolfgang and to target the music to specific audiences. I guess this is for those of us who aren't quite sure what we want from Mozart: I don't know what'll it be — raise my IQ or take a power nap?

The Marketed Mozart CDs start in the crib: *Mozart for Mothers-to-be* or *Baby Needs Mozart.* Not only does research show that Mozart is a favorite with babies six months and older, the maestro will give your little one a head start in life and school and an edge in our increasingly competitive world — and it works on parents, too.

For those of us who just want to get smarter, we could choose from *Tune Your Brain with Mozart, More Mozart for Your Mind* or *Better Thinking Through Mozart.*

For an artistic pick-me-up, I'd try *Music for the Mozart Effect,* which aids creativity and inspiration.

The CD's are packaged for different times of day. There's *Mozart in the Morning* right through to *Mozart at Midnight* which can be used either as prelude to sleep or a companion to late night/early morning activities. Is our boy versatile or what?

For the more specific-minded shopper, Mozart is packaged for a range of activities, beginning with Mozart for *Morning Meditation* or *Mozart for the Morning Commute.* ("This is a lively bit of traveling music," the CD jacket tells us, " to speed you on your way.")

Mozart for Massage is tempting, but my favorite is *Mozart on the Menu* with what is described as "delectable music" for any social event — brunch, candlelit dinner for two, or a quiet midnight snack. This CD has organized Mozart by the course. For the Appetizer, there's *Einekleina Nachtmusic;* for the main course, the *Flute Quintet in D* and the *Oboe Concerto in C;* and for dessert, may we suggest the *String Quartet in E Flat.* Live it up and have brandy and a cigar afterwards.

And this was only Mozart. I talked about this to some of my musician friends — professional, classical musicians. One of them hazarded a guess that because the field of music therapy is so new, the research has been done only on Mozart. (Oh, those pesky college students and those slugabed ethnomusicologists/radio personalities, dogging it on the research.)

Still, I know there is something valid in it. On my quest to simplify and calm my life, classical music has been one of the most powerful influences. I still listen to Van Morrison or Bob Marley to rev up energy when I'm cooking or cleaning house, but when I'm working diligently at my desk, the most productive music for me is Bach, Haydn or Mozart. "Of course," said Anna, a concert pianist, "because of the constant rhythms in Bach and the steady, measured pulse.

Not the surges of later romantic composers like Tchaikovsky"

Yeah. That's what I thought.

So I took a simple survey. I asked my musician friends about other mood-altering composers. Who would you recommend, I asked them, for some mood, mind and body pick-me-ups? Here's what they said:

- For energy — Bach, especially the orchestral suites
- For efficiency — again Bach
- For determination — Elgar, so pompous and English
- For creativity — Brahms or Mozart piano concertos
- For intelligence — Mozart, Beethoven or a big Bach triple fugue
- For good cheer — Mozart quintets or French woodwind music
- For relaxation — Debussy
- And, during the Christmas season, for a heart-warming, anti-Scrooge mood it was unanimous — Beethoven.

Finally, I asked them to recommend one great, uplifting piece of classical music for the holiday season. They gave two great recommendations, either Rachmaninoff's *Second Piano Concerto* or Beethoven's *Emperor Concerto.*

Or, we could always go back to the pre-packaged and target-marketed Mozart. An all-purpose, one-size-fits-all CD, perhaps. How about the one titled *Mozart's Greatest Hits?* That oughta cover the musical waterfront.

PEARL BUCK, STORYTELLER

December is the season of stories. This time of year we revisit and revere our cultural stories — the birth of a baby in a manger, a little girl named Clara with a wooden nutcracker, a little lame boy named Tiny Tim. These are stories of transformation, miracles from ordinary beginnings.

In families, too, it's the time to celebrate stories — the Christmas all the five-year-old cousins had chickenpox, the year my father brought home a live goose to fatten and eat, but my sister and I named it Gregory and made it a pet instead.

Our enduring societal fondness for stories reminds me of the life of a renowned storyteller, the writer Pearl Buck. I gave a book review at the Central Library when her biography[1] came out and I began by asking the question, "How many of you have read something by Pearl Buck?" About a hundred people were in the audience and every hand but two went up.

Pearl Buck was born in the United States in 1892 but grew up in China where her parents were missionaries. The Celestial Empire did not welcome foreigners. They considered anyone who was not Chinese to be barbaric, scarcely more than animals. Most Chinese believed that the missionaries had come to find slaves, smelled bad, worshipped a pig and ate Chinese children. In this hostile climate, with a father she considered a religious fanatic, she had a lonely childhood, became a missionary's wife, had an unhappy marriage and an affair with a Chinese poet who was killed in a plane crash. She was almost forty before anything she wrote was published. It was the beginning of a phenomenally successful career. During her lifetime, no American author, with the possible exception of Mark Twain, has been translated more than Pearl Buck.

Her second book was *The Good Earth*, published in 1931; it was an immediate bestseller. She was still in China when she was notified that it was chosen to be a Book of the Month Club selection. She was so naïve she wrote back, "I'm pleased if you are, but do they know I'm not a member of their club?" After the publication of that book, her life changed forever. She moved to the United States, remarried (her editor and publisher) and became a celebrity. In the mid-1930s, the depth of the Depression, she earned $50,000 to $70,000 a year.

She was the most influential Westerner to write about China since Marco Polo in the eighteenth century. The difference between writing fiction in the East and in the West, she said, was that of originality. In Chinese literature, authors are often unknown and the work is a collection of folk tales gathered over time. This form is more like life, she said, because life has no plot or subplot. We meet people, our lives coincide for a time, then they walk out of the story and we never see them again or know their end, any more than we know our own.

Pearl Buck's career was as long as it was successful. Not only was she the author of popular works, she won both the Pulitzer Prize and the Nobel Prize for literature. She wrote more than seventy books, many of them bestsellers. She wrote novels, short stories, plays, biographies, translations from Chinese, children's literature, essays, journalism and poetry. In a rigid schedule of self-discipline, she wrote every morning, about 2,500 words a day, eight to twelve handwritten pages with few revisions. Her lyrical style was highly praised. She said it came from the stories she heard from her Chinese nanny and from the King James Bible.

Until I read her biography, I didn't know that she was also a political reformer and ahead of her time on issues such as birth control, women's rights, anti-Communism, child welfare and racial equal rights. She was one of the few Americans who spoke out strongly against the U.S. internment of Japanese-Americans during World War II. The FBI kept a surveillance file on her until the end of her life.

In person, she was quiet and shy — "a brown hen," she described herself — but when championing a cause, and especially a cause of injustice, she became, she said, "excruciatingly articulate."

It was as a writer and storyteller that Pearl Buck was most famous. One Gallup Poll showed she was one of the ten most admired women in America. Then she became an invisible woman in literature. Some said it was because she was too popular, too successful, too prolific. Later, critics and college professors scorned her. They didn't teach her work or include it in survey books of American literature. Her work lacked complexity and objectivity, they said. Others said her fall from grace was because she was a woman writer, because she wrote about women and Asians and because her tremendous popularity affronted intellectuals.

But as I learned when I gave my book review, people still love her work. Many had personal stories to tell about the time they met her or heard her speak. She endures because she wrote about the importance of family, the land that sustains us and the passing of life from one generation to another.

I was invited to give the book review again, at a nursing home. The audience that day turned out to be only about a dozen women, old and ill. Again I began by asking, "How many of you have read anything by Pearl Buck?" Most of them were either dozing or medicated, so only one hand went up.

"Okay," I said, putting away my notes of dates and publications and quotes, "tell you what let's do. I'll tell you some stores about her life." And I did and we all had a great time because that's what we love, isn't it, the stories we share.

1. Pearl Buck: *A Cultural Biography,* Peter Con., Cambridge University Press, 1996

REAL HEROES

I once met a woman at a New York party who had known Lillian Hellman quite well and who told me, in the course of our conversation, that Ms. Hellman's memoirs, which were very popular at the time, were not all true. Either they were exaggerated or the stories she told didn't happen to her. I could not have been more shocked, although I don't know why. A person writing autobiography isn't under oath. I think the literary phrase for that is "reinventing oneself." Besides, we should know better than to believe fiction writers. They write fiction.

I recently discovered the hugely popular book *The Education of Little Tree* by Forrest Carter, which was published twenty years ago. It's sort of an Indian Huckleberry Finn about a little orphaned boy and his grandparents in the Eastern Cherokee hill country.

Now, there's a movie based on the book. One review of the movie referred to a controversy that had tainted the book. I felt like Dorothy tumbling head over heels into an Oz of discovery. A book? A movie? A controversy?

So I went to the library to read about Forrest Carter, who was part Cherokee, orphaned at ten, raised by his grandparents, never spent more than six months in a classroom, said he learned everything he knew in a public library, spent most of his life working as a ranch hand and wood chopper and was forty before he realized his dream of becoming a writer. He wrote a story, published it himself, sent it to Hollywood agents and actors and it became the movie *The Outlaw Josey Wales* starring Clint Eastwood. Mr.

Carter dedicated each of his subsequent books to a different Indian tribe and donated a significant portion of his earnings to Indian causes. He died in 1979.

The controversy over *The Education of Little Tree* came some time later when someone claimed that Mr. Carter was a Ku Klux Klansman who wrote the story in atonement. The book had been out for years. Then it won an award, and a professor in New Jersey or somewhere unearthed the author's past and all hell broke loose. Mr. Carter was dead by now and unable to defend himself against cheap shots.

The foreword to the book was written by Rennard Strickland, an expert in Indian literature, history and law. So I called him and asked him the true story.

"No," Dr. Strickland said, "Mr. Carter was not a Klansman. But he had worked as a speechwriter for George Wallace. And remember, the Cherokees were slave-holding Indians."

Dr. Strickland, a university professor and dean, was called for interviews from everybody from New York publications to the BBC. One white-haired lady waited for him after a speech he said.

"I want to talk to you about all this fuss," she said, and Dr. Strickland braced himself for an attack. "Even if it were true," she said, "don't they think people can change?"

What has not changed is the popularity of the book. When it was reissued, the University of New Mexico Press considered a new foreword referring to the brouhaha, but decided against it. The only change they made was to take the word "autobiography" off the title page.

I am of Cherokee heritage and have read a lot of Indian history, but this book told me something I didn't know — that the Trail of Tears was not called that by the Indians. It was too tragic for tears, they said. It was the people who watched them on that death march who named it. Although the soldiers provided some wagons, Forrest Carter wrote, the Indians, silent in protest, would not ride. They walked the entire way. They would not even put their dead in the wagons and when they were not permitted to stop and bury them, they carried the bodies in their arms. And the people watching the exodus wept for them.

Dr. Strickland told me another story. He said that for writing the foreword, he was offered either a small percentage of royalties or $200. He took the $200 and it seemed like a good deal at the time. "We didn't know it was going to be such a big success," he laughed. The first edition was only about 5,000 and it didn't sell. The book was remaindered. But it's been selling ever since and now *The Education of Little Tree* by Forrest Carter has sold more than a million copies.

This is from the book: "Gramma said when you come on something good, first thing to do is share it with whoever you can find; that way, the good spreads out where no telling it will go. Which is right."

By the way, when he got the $200, Dr. Strickland, who is also an author, donated it to the University of New Mexico Press.

I once interviewed the great Hollywood stuntman Yakima Canutt for a magazine story I was writing about him. He was a former rodeo champion who taught movie cowboys how to be he-men. He worked with Tom Mix, he taught Gene Autry how to ride a horse, he taught Roy Rogers how to throw a punch, he taught Charlton Heston how to drive a chariot. John Wayne copied his rolling walk and drawling talk to become the epitome of the Western hero.

Yakima Cannut's most famous stunt, and one that has never been duplicated, was in the 1939 movie *Stagecoach*. He fell among the galloping team of six horses, clung to the wooden shaft amid those thundering hoofs, then let go and dropped to the ground as the horses and stagecoach passed over him. I have an autographed picture of that stunt.

The stunt was so spectacular, he got a $1,000 bonus.

"That was a lot of money in 1939," I said.

"Little lady," he replied, "that was a lot of stunt."

Cowboys or Indians or writers, the hero is the person who really does the stunt.

WHATEVER HAPPENED TO MR. DARCY?

The old saw "Every cloud has a silver lining" certainly wasn't coined in Oklahoma in the summer, where we go for weeks without seeing any cloud, lined or unlined. An old-timer told me about an infamous Oklahoma drought. "It was so hot and so dry for so long," she said, "when the weather finally did break, even the cat stood out in the rain."

I did find a silver lining to last summer's heat and drought and it's this: After weeks of feeling as though I was living inside a Hasty Bake oven, I lost all interest in the garden and came inside with a stack of books. I read biographies, lost in the lives and times of three fascinating artists: Jane Austen, Catherine Cookson and Elvis Presley. I know, strange trio. At first glance they would appear to be unimaginably dissimilar. But what these biographies have in common is that all three are stories of individuals with an artistic gift and such a powerful drive to express it that they broke out of the restraints of their time and society, much like plants fighting through asphalt toward the sunlight. Their stories are the account of what that struggle cost them. These books also show us the difference between the tabloids peeping-through-the-windows at celebrities and good biographies that not only tell a whopping good story, but teach and touch us as readers. They tell us something about this mysterious family of humanity.

Catherine Cookson was an English novelist, so enormously popular I was surprised that I hadn't read any of her books. I first learned of her when I read her obituary. She was a prolific writer who wrote almost 100 novels before she died at the age of ninety-one. She was born in 1906 in northern England near Newcastle, an illegitimate child in a family of bleak, grimy poverty. Her biography tells of a precocious but outcast little girl in an alcoholic family shackled by grinding labor. At twenty-two, a beau ended their romance because of her lower class and, with a broken heart, she left her hometown, found a job in the workhouse laundry and miraculously scrimped and saved enough to buy a fifteen room house of her own. She married a schoolmaster, suffered four miscarriages or stillbirths, had a nervous breakdown, was confined to a psychiatric hospital and provided for her difficult, alcoholic mother. She began writing at age forty. Her work became her salvation. Every day she cleaned her entire house — often without the aid of electricity or running water — before beginning work on her novels. She wrote about the working class and hardscrabble lives, creating characters who struggle not only to survive but also to make sense of survival. At the time of her death, she was a best-selling contemporary author, honored by the Queen with the female equivalent of knighthood. She was born poor and lower class, but she died titled Dame Catherine Cookson.

I started reading *Last Train to Memphis: The Rise of Elvis Presley* out of a sense of duty because the author, Peter Guralnick, and I were going to be on a panel at a writers' conference. Once I started it, I couldn't stop reading it and I understood why this biography has been described as "the first great rock-and-roll biography" and "a masterpiece" and, according to the *The New York*

Times, "a triumph of biographical art."

It is a 488-page book that covers only the first twenty-three years of Elvis Presley's life; the second volume is 767 pages. How, I asked myself, bleary-eyed from compulsive reading, can this book be so compelling? How can there be anything we don't already know about Elvis Presley, at least anything we care to know? The answer is that the book, like the story of the singer himself, is an American epic. It's not only the story of a poor country boy of great ambition and fiery musical passions, and of a wounded life that spins out of control, but it's also the story of the times — America in the 1950s and how that postwar era spawned cultural heroes such as James Dean, Marlon Brando, and Presley.

Jane Austen, born in 1775, the daughter of a clergyman, supposedly was a sheltered, poor spinster who lived all her life with her parents and sister in a quiet English village, often in a house provided by a brother, and who died at age forty-one. She was the author of six novels, about half of them published after her death. The biography *Jane Austen: A Life* by Claire Tomalin was highly praised and, since it was just out in paperback (Vintage Books, 1999), I couldn't resist. *The New Yorker* called this book "a page turner." Frankly I wondered what could possibly be written about her that I haven't read in a handful of previous biographies because I am a Jane Austen aficionado.

Ah, ye of little faith and much vanity. No wonder the book was a *New York Times* Notable Book of the Year. Ms. Tomalin is a skillful biographer who has unearthed some new information and has written the life with such a gift of storytelling that it is as exhilarating as a tingling mystery. Neither Ms. Austen nor her era were as sheltered as we might have supposed. She knew something about the world, its wars and ways. There's a new theory about her death, new information about her failed romances, a strongly supported theory that the reason Ms. Austen wrote nothing for ten years after a burst of creativity was clinical depression. What makes the book riveting is that it transports us with vivid detail to another time and place, a time when the Napoleonic war boiled, when the English class structure extended to morals and childrearing, and when family life was often severed by death in childbirth.

Ever since I saw the BBC-TV and A&E series of *Pride and Prejudice*, I've been worried about Mr. Darcy and Elizabeth Bennet. It's a satisfying romantic fantasy to think of Elizabeth Bennet, from the gentry class, marrying Fitzwilliam Darcy, of the nobility. Colin Firth portrayed Mr. Darcy with stunning appeal; one review said he "smoldered" through the role. But here's what I wonder; what kind of husband is he going to be when he stops smoldering and starts complaining about his in-laws, which we all know he will. After all, a central theme of the novel is knowing the difference between appearance and real character.

I remember a "Dear Abby" letter from a woman who signed herself "Tired of Living with a Grouch." The prognosis, Abby replied, was not good. My secret fear is that Mr. Darcy will become a grump and that he and the outspoken Elizabeth will spend their married life verbally sniping at one another.

Then I discovered an extraordinary little book by Fay Weldon entitled *Letters to Alice on First Reading Jane Austen*. It's a modern writer's passionate reply to a niece's complaint that Jane Austen is tedious and not relevant to the contemporary reader. It has become one of my favorite books of all time. It is witty, lively and informative about reading and writing fiction; the parts about Jane Austen's work and world tear your heart out.

Pride and Prejudice is a novel about love and marriage and finding husbands for five daughters. Ms. Weldon's book is about the grim reality of a woman's life in eighteenth century England. Yank the bonnet off of pretty Regency England and the hard facts were: legal sexism, malnutrition, ignorance, death and infant mortality. If the children had pink cheeks, Ms. Weldon writes, its because they had tuberculosis. Fifty percent of all babies died before the age of two.

Marriage was virtually the only occupation available to women at the time, according to Ms. Weldon, but only thirty percent of women married, because the other seventy percent couldn't afford to. Women had to have a dowry. If they didn't have one, no use waiting for their parents to die to inherit because by law all property went to the men in the family. Women could inherit only from their husbands and sometimes not then. Any property acquired during marriage belonged to the husband. The children were considered his, not hers.

Ms. Weldon takes a kind view of the nervous Mrs. Bennet in *Pride and Prejudice*; she sympathizes with a mother of five marriageable daughters barred by law from being citizens of the economy. If their father died, they would all be unprovided for.

A woman who was born poor, stayed poor and lived with her parents or other relatives all of her life. No respectable woman lived alone. If she did marry, she'd better hope it was happy because marriage was forever. Between the years 1650 and 1850 there were only 250 divorces in England, about one divorce a year.

There was virtually no birth control, so marriage meant lots of pregnancies, many miscarriages and childbirth. A woman typically had fifteen pregnancies, six of those brought to term, with one in four being stillborn. The fifty percent child mortality was attributed to disease, infection, malnutrition and ignorance. It was ignorance about calcium that caused a woman to lose her teeth in pregnancy; traditionally, one tooth for every child she bore. Jane Austen's mother had eight children and according to a cousin, had lost a number of front teeth which made her look old.

Jane Austen never married or had children. She put on her cap at age thirty, which declared she was off the marriage market. All of her life, Ms. Austen was sorely aware of being the poor relation. Publication of her books and the prospect of money of her own must have given her a dizzying sense of independence. She died six years later in 1817, still living in her mother's home. Her father had died some years before and left the family unprovided for.

On the bright side, the countryside of Regency England was very pretty.

When Jane Austen wrote that it was better not to marry at all than to marry without love, she was writing fiction. It was a new notion at the time, according to Ms. Weldon, and it gave us a legacy to build up.

After reading *Letters to Alice*, I feel even more tenderness for Jane Austen's characters. I hope Mr. Darcy did not turn into a stay-at-home grump and that he smoldered throughout their life together. I hope when Elizabeth became Mrs. Darcy, she stayed bright, independent and in love. And I hope that she kept all her teeth.

The Girl from Leam Lane: The Life and Writing of Catherine Cookson, Piers Dudgeon, Headline Bk Pub Ltd, 1998

EVERYTHING I NEED TO KNOW I LEARNED AT THE BALLET

Who among the literate public doesn't know about the best-selling book *Everything I Need to Know I Learned in Kindergarten?* The title alone became an Americana catchphrase and the book inspired a slew of other books including one I like titled, *Everything I Need to Know I Learned from My Cat.*

It's such a catchy title, someone has probably written a book like that on every subject. In fact, I wrote one myself. It's called *Everything I Need to Know I Learned at the Ballet.*

I worked at a ballet company for fifteen years and my book includes some of the life lessons I observed in a mix of wisdom and humor. It's Miss Manners in pointe shoes. The book offers advice and morals, such as:

- Don't Drop Your Partner on the Floor.
- Be Nice to Someone Littler Than You.
- When the Curtain Comes Down, Stop Performing.

Each was to be illustrated with a drawing of a winsome young dancer. The message of the book is that there are valuable lessons to be learned in a ballet studio that can serve us elsewhere in life. Lessons about self-discipline, teamwork, mental concentration, good manners and hard work.

The same could be said about team sports or civic organizations, but I wrote it about ballet, an art of near obsessive self-discipline.

Sadly, my book was never published because of the illustrations. Or, to be accurate, the lack of illustrations. The publisher thought that the illustrations were half of the charm. That's what the publisher thought — half. I thought, more like forty percent, maybe thirty. To me, the text was the important part. That was the part I did. Anyway, the illustrator pulled out of the project and publication never happened.

I can understand why a publisher doesn't want to publish an illustrated book without illustrations, but that didn't make it less painful for me. After all, I'd done my part. The book was my idea. I found the illustrator; I invited her to participate. This was not fair. This was not fun. This was much like ballet itself.

Now here's the bitter irony. The illustrator, or rather the non-illustrator, is a retired dancer and the reason she couldn't do the work for this ballet book was because an old dance injury was bothering her. O, twist the knife! Hadn't she read the text? The part about not dropping your partner on the floor? The part about commitment? Those are some of my favorite parts.

So, there is no published book titled *Everything I Need to Know I Learned at the Ballet*. I suppose now I can say there is something else I have learned at the ballet — that you can't dance a *pas de deux* alone. Either have a back-up partner, or be prepared to do a solo. Or, accept the fact that in the arts, as in life, the program is subject to change. I guess these are things I need to know, but they are not things I wanted to learn.

ADVICE TO A YOUNG WRITER

I began reading George Plimpton's biography of Truman Capote with some misgivings because of the format. It is an oral biography, no narrative, just people telling stories about Capote. It struck me as a lazy way of writing a book, but I was wrong. Again. The eyewitness accounts build upon one another and become so compelling I could hardly tear myself away from it.

The writers particularly — Gore Vidal, Norman Mailer, Capote himself — were articulate, observant, funny and vicious in the stories they told about one another. Lillian Hellman was one of the writers they savaged with glee. She described herself as a fierce warrior of justice, but Mailer said she was really a celebrity lover, and lover is not the word he used. "It must be said of Lillian," Mailer said, "that when the chips were down she'd always go for the guy who had the most clout." Capote said that she looked like George Washington in drag.

So I should have been prepared for the worst when an article — written by a writer — appeared in *The New York Review of Books* about my heroine, Angie Debo. I expected it to be completely favorable; self-delusion is a tough bug to shake.

I first met Dr. Debo in 1975 at the University of Tulsa. I was an employee there and she was the guest speaker for a special occasion. I had not heard of her before and was ashamed of my ignorance. Dr. Debo is known as the First Lady of Oklahoma History. She is a nationally recognized scholar and author, a pioneer in the field of Indian history. She wrote and edited thirteen books and hundreds of articles. She was the first woman to have her portrait hung in the State Capitol, among the state's other historical treasures such as Jim Thorpe, Sequoyah and Will Rogers. She did most of this work from Marshall, Oklahoma, where the population hovered around 400.

That spring day at TU, sitting on the back row of a big auditorium, I was moved to tears by her speech and by the intensity, integrity and accomplishments of this tiny woman with a fluff of white hair who could barely see over the podium. I was impressed that, four years earlier, her book, *A History of the Indians of the United States,* had been reviewed jointly in *The New York Times* with Dee Brown's *Bury My Heart at Wounded Knee*. The country was experiencing a spike in the championing of Indians, a recurring national phenomenon that alternates with ignoring them altogether.

She spoke that day about the importance of integrity for writers, whether they were writing nonfiction or poetry. And she ground what I would learn was one of her favorite axes, criticizing both John Steinbeck and Edna Ferber for writing blatant inaccuracies about Oklahoma. Steinbeck never spent five minutes in the state she said, but Ferber said she spent thirteen days in Oklahoma researching her topic. "Personally I think she could have learned more in thirteen days," Dr. Debo said, "but perhaps she was a slow learner."

I repeated this story to the Doubleday senior editor who had been Ferber's editor, and he was not amused. "Edna Ferber was not slow," he snapped.

Steinbeck and Ferber wrote memorable characters

and situations, Dr. Debo said, but they were ignorant about the physical and historical setting of Oklahoma — the land, geology, history, and Indian policy. "It would be like writing a novel about the Civil War and setting it in Alaska," she said. Barbara Kingsolver is lucky that Dr. Debo did not read her novel *Pigs in Heaven,* which was highly praised yet set in a place that doesn't exist — a Cherokee reservation in desert Oklahoma.

Dr. Debo and I began a correspondence immediately after her TU talk. That was the beginning of a friendship that lasted thirteen years until she died in 1988 at age ninety-eight. She became my close friend and mentor. When we first met, she was eighty-five and I was thirty-two. I have a big box of letters, audiotapes and notes of phone calls and visits with her in Marshall and in Tulsa. In Marshall, the townspeople call her Miss Angie. I never called her by her first name. I always referred to her as Dr. Debo. It is a term of respect, with a dollop of deference to our fifty-year age difference. Many of her letters to me begin with the salutation, Beloved Young Friend.

Dr. Debo lived most of her life in Marshall in a little white house her brother had built in the 1920s, but she had seen something of the wider world. She supported the education of a young girl in Uganda whom she met there, she had ridden a camel in Egypt, studied in Europe and visited Alaska. Her Christmas letter of 1969 talked about the war in Vietnam and how to write congressmen and senators about the land issue of Alaskan natives. From her home, she took her role of citizen seriously and directed active and effective campaigns to correct abuses of native tribes. "It began with the unresolved land claim of the Eskimos, Indians and Aleuts of Alaska," she wrote in an article titled "To Establish Justice". Then she began to include information in her annual Christmas letter to friends, summarizing bills and developments in Washington, advising action and asking her correspondents to each write six letters to public officials. Her mailing list grew to hundreds. "I bought postage stamps like wallpaper," she said, "but I know of no better way of spending money."

The deep current of our communication was about writing: good writing, accuracy in writing, careers in writing, writing and being female, writing and being married (she chose not to marry), writing and holding another job, dreams and disappointments that wound the heart and, through it all, the hard work and the love for the work of writing. She was encouraging, but also direct and straight-shooting in her criticism. "Not your best work," she told me after reading a magazine article I had written.

Over the years, I have given many talks about her, and, on a couple of occasions, for her when she could not accept the invitation because of poor health. I wrote several magazine articles about her and one with her. After her death in January, 1995, I was asked to appear on a panel at Oklahoma State University commemorating the fiftieth anniversary of her classic book, *Prairie City, the Story of an American Community.* I dipped into my box of memories and discovered that I had a larger collection of letters from her than anyone, even the Angie Debo Collection at OSU. I quoted excerpts of her letters to me and titled that talk, "Advice to a Young Writer."

The advice she gave me came from her own writing career. She talked about:

◗ **Disappointment,** with a lesson that came from the publication of *Prairie City* (A.A.Knopf, New York, 1944). "That book never got the attention it deserved," she wrote me. "Nobody bought it and Knopf remaindered it ... it was the only book I ever had remaindered." What she learned from that experience, she told me, is that "it is important to keep writing books, even if no one is interested."

Prairie City was reissued in 1967 and again in 1985.

◗ **Discrimination.** "I am very sensitive to persons not getting the opportunity they deserve," she wrote. "It's disgusting."

She was a trailblazer in writing Indian history. Her first Indian book was published in 1934, so long ago that it was the era of silent movies when Ken Maynard was King of the Westerns.

She became a writer because the academic world was closed to her. She had wanted to be a teacher since she was a girl of six on the raw prairie. "Teachers walked in grandeur among us," she said. This was her life's goal, but she found the field was barred to female teachers. She was graduated from the prestigious University of Chicago in 1924 with a master's degree in history, impressive academic credentials. No university would hire a woman. "Thirty calls came in that spring to the history department," she wrote. "One of the thirty said they would take a woman if no men were available; the other twenty-nine said they wouldn't take a woman under any circumstances. You can imagine the effect on us . . . Here was an immovable wall in front of me and I could not breach it."

She chose the obscure subject of Indians for her doctoral dissertation because her advisor suggested she write a history of the Choctaws. "It was not any more romantic than that," she wrote. The dissertation was published as *The Rise and Fall of the Choctaw Republic* (University of Oklahoma Press, Norman OK, 1934, reissued 1961). It was awarded the John H. Dunning Prize as the best book submitted in any field of American history that year. Based on that, "I took a chance," she said, "and cut loose for free-lance writing." She described the "fear and dreading" of her decision. "I was betting my life, and I mean that literally, on what I believed was the right thing to do, the proper way to use what gifts I had."

At first, in the lean economy of the Depression, it seemed she had made a grave mistake. She had two unpublished manuscripts. "One was the most important writing I had ever done (*And Still the Waters Run*) and the other was the best I could do in an entirely new field (*The Road to Disappearance*, a history of the Creek Indians.)" It was a time of desperate discouragement. She was forty-four years old.

Eventually, both manuscripts were published and her life changed. "And I found my work stood entirely on its merits ... I cannot tell you the sense of liberation it gave me ... fair field and no favors — all I ever asked. During the years since, I have stopped writing for a time to do other things ... but writing has been my real job."

◗ **Integrity.** The manuscript that gave her the most trouble, she said, was *Oklahoma: Foot-loose and Fancy-free* (University of Oklahoma Press, Norman OK, 1949, reissued 1982), an interpretation of the spirit of the state. There were raging battles about editing. She would submit to deletions but never to additions written by editors. When the book came out, it was highly praised without any adverse comments by reviewers. "It taught me one thing," she said, "to write to please myself. If it doesn't please a publisher, try another."

At 5' 1/2" and 110 pounds, she seemed an unlikely warrior, but she was a ferocious fighter for truth and accuracy. Decades later, she would still rail about an "ignoramus" editor who added erroneous statements to one of her manuscripts. Then she would laugh and say, "You can't have a battle of wits with an unarmed man."

◗ **Courage.** Her most important book, she maintained, was *And Still the Waters Run* (Princeton University Press, 1930, Princeton, New Jersey. Reprinted 1966, 1972.) It is the meticulously researched account of the liquidation of the Five Civilized Tribes in Oklahoma. "It remains the premier work about exploitation of Indian lands," wrote a contemporary Indian law expert, "and is still cited by courts of law as the definitive record of that tragic episode in American history."

Dr. Debo discovered corruption in social, government and religious organizations. "Everything I touched about that story was slimy," she said. When she was doing her solitary research in basement archives, she said, she had such a feeling of crime that it was "an instinctive feeling of fear." She uncovered and wrote about the involvement of prominent Oklahomans, naming names of guilty legislators. The manuscript was so explosive, it threatened to destroy the OU Press as legislators would surely retaliate and cut off funding, so she withdrew the manuscript. She waited, trying to find another publisher. Four years later, the director of the

OU Press resigned, became director of the Princeton University Press and the first book he published was *And Still the Waters Run.* When the book came out, she said, "There was not one yip of protest, because it was true."

Ironically, she never intended to be pro-Indian or pro-anything, she said, except pro-integrity. "My one goal was to discover the truth and publish it."

◗ **Hard work comes first.** She was both delighted and amused by the acclaim she received late in life. "I have told more unpleasant tales about this state than anyone who ever tapped out the name on a typewriter," she laughed.

Early in our friendship I had an idea for a statewide birthday celebration for her, a scheme which entertained her enormously. "I love you for being so young and ardent," she wrote me. "I do write with integrity and occasionally, but not often, with a certain felicity of expression. It pleased me that you overestimate my — ahem — fame. . . . Nothing I write ever sounds good to me until it's so old I've forgotten it, then I read it and think, Was I ever good enough to write like that?... I do love good writing. It gives me a lift like looking at a rose or listening to a mockingbird."

Some of the personal stories she told me were hard for her to share and had been devastating to her as a young professional. What saved her, I believe, was writing and her commitment to hard work. She told me those stories because she was courageous, because she wanted to pass on her wisdom and because she wanted to encourage me and other young writers.

In 1975, in one of her first letters to me, she

wrote, "I shall not be writing much more. It gives me great pleasure to meet young and gifted people who will carry on. For there are many things to be written about and you will be writing them ... and I shall be reading them."

Her last book, and one of her best, was *Geronimo: The Man, His Place, His Time* (University of Oklahoma Press, 1976, Norman OK), published when she was eighty-seven. "If anyone asked me to write another book," she said, "I'd sic the dogs on them. If I had any dogs."

Dr. Debo had been dead almost a decade when Larry McMurtry wrote his article about her work. It appeared in the Oct. 23, 1997, issue of *The New York Review of Books*. He praised her first-class intellect, her self-made career, her reputation and especially her trilogy of Oklahoma Indian histories and her biography of Geronimo. But then he wrote, "In her mid-nineties she finally became cute. She bought herself a black bonnet and took to dressing like Queen Victoria, at least on state occasions."

I wrote him a letter correcting his impression. Ever since *Prairie City* had come out, the town of Marshall had an annual Prairie City Days celebration with a parade. The grand marshal was the town's celebrity, Miss Angie, who wore territorial costume for the occasion — a long, black dress and an antique black hat. She showed me the clothing; it had belonged to her mother. McMurtry must have seen a photo of that event and leapt to the wrong conclusion.

He replied with a gracious note.

What appeased me was not his reply so much as discovering what another famous writer had said about her and the importance of her work. Mari Sandoz had written an enthusiastic review of *Prairie City* for *The New York Times:*

"A people without history is like the wind on buffalo grass."

Still, this has made me edgy about something in my own life. There are photos of me with the cast of *CATS* at a Halloween party in a makeshift cat costume. So I wonder, will someone look at those pictures one day and declare: Connie loved cats and, later in her life, she came to think she was a cat.

Perhaps that will be one of the nicest things they could say about me.

PARTY OF ONE

It was a staff meeting to boost morale. Our busy season was throttling us and we were all tired, overworked, underpaid, stressed, sick or all of the above. So there was food and a little contest with a prize at this staff meeting.

"What we're going to do," I said brightly, "is tell about the worst job we ever had. We'll go around the table and then there's a prize for the all-time worst."

"Me first," said Nora from the ticket office. "One summer I was a barf girl."

"A what?"

"Barf girl. At an amusement park. Whenever a kid got sick on one of the rides, I'm the one they called to clean it up."

A silence like a lead pipe hit the staff.

After a while someone said dryly, "Okay. What's another game we can play?"

The barf girl won the prize so fast and so hard, the rest of us weren't even in the contest. We ate cookies in silence and meditated quietly about bad jobs we'd had — our current one included, most of us thought.

I've been lucky with jobs. I have stumbled into a series of interesting jobs. When I interviewed for the job at the ballet company, I showed the committee my portfolio and talked about what I thought I could do for the company, and then I said, "Besides that, I am wearing Pavlova perfume. I hope you take that into consideration." They burst into laughter and hired me. They thought the job needed someone with a sense of humor.

Here's how I slid into the job of doing commentaries on public radio station KWGS. I ran into general manager Rich Fisher at Ron's Hamburgers, a classic diner with a red countertop and ten stools.

"Drop by the station sometime and do a commentary" he said on his way out the door.

I did, and the staff was too polite to tell me not to come back, so I kept doing them. Shows you that a five-star bowl of chili can redirect the course of destiny.

I like the breezy, essay style of commentaries. I like the intimacy of radio and the programming of public radio.

In the commentaries I talk about things I've discovered while downshifting from a workaholic life that roared along like a roller derby. I'm learning to amble and saunter instead of sprint and dogtrot. I think the rule for jogging is that if you can talk as you run, you're not pushing too hard. The rule for the other side of the street is that if you're not asleep, you're not going too slowly.

My commentaries are like chatting at lunch with friends: family, hair, aging (them and us), books, vacations, shopping, pop culture, gripes, broken hearts and funny stories. With friends, you share your wisdom and pool your ignorance. I'm lucky to have friends who can talk about something besides the St. John fashion show, friends who can laugh at themselves and at me. The only thing remarkable about my everyday discoveries is that they're mine. That counts. The Irish, such a lyrical and poetic people, have a maxim about that: *There's no sore ass like your own sore ass.*

After a certain age, my friend Patti said, we want

patterned china, cement in the yard and diamonds. We want real diamonds, but we also want other kinds of jewels.

When I heard a priest begin a sermon, "Once when I was living on an Indian reservation in South Dakota . . ." I was puce with envy at her rich life experience. "I can't say anything like that," I lamented to a friend.

"Sure you can," he replied. "You can say, "Once when I was shopping in Utica Square ..."

I love stories from colorful lives. I read to discover nuggets such as James Joyce, that wag, saying he liked blackberry jam because it was the blackberry bush that supplied the thorns for Christ's crown. Or to read that Degas, revered as the master, went to the 1911 Paris exhibition of Ingres every day. He was very old and blind, so he couldn't see the paintings. He went to touch them in veneration.

All lives are adventures, it's just that some are in the Pyrenees and some are in the backyard. What's important is that they are our adventures and that we mine them. Harry Truman said, "The only things I learned worth knowing are the things I learned after I knew it all."

I've often been a loner, but one of the hardest lessons I learned was about solitude. Being alone, and doing it comfortably and well, seems to be a learned skill, like playing the banjo. It starts with the reason for being alone. By choice or by loss? To work or to rest? A job or a move or a change in your life? Those factors influence how we feel about being alone and sometimes it's with shame, pain, sorrow or anger.

Change is hard for me. I go through change like a cartoon cat, clawing and scratching at the doorframe. Once on the other side, I am thrilled to be there, but that grateful recognition can be a long time coming. I believe the universe takes us where we need to be, but I keep forgetting that I believe that.

I can remember times in my life when I was mortified not to have a date on Friday night, or to be seen shopping for groceries on Saturday evening, or even to take solitary walks. I felt as if I were wearing floppy clown shoes, a red nose and trailing a neon sign that said "Poor, tragic me."

We want to step out bravely into the world. Some occasions are tougher to go it alone than others. Going to a concert or a play alone? Okay. Eating out alone? Sometimes hard, especially if you force yourself not to take a book. Going to small parties alone? Okay. Going to a big reception alone? Hard. On a vacation trip alone? Scary. Going to a ball alone? Nuts.

"We need time to dream, to remember, time to be," said writer Gladys Tabor.

We have many words to describe the different moods of being alone. Solitude is celebrated, especially by creative people. "Loneliness is the poverty of self," May Sarton wrote, "solitude is the richness of self." I first saw the possibility of joy in being alone when I read May Sarton's journals, especially *Plant Dreaming Deep.* I have come to cherish my solitude and to protect it fiercely. That's not always easy to do, especially when the tribe around you is clamoring for you to get busy.

Being alone is in sharp focus during holidays. "How was the Christmas holidays?" I asked a single person and his answer was sad. "It's just another day to me," he said. "It's just me."

I hope I never use the phrase "just me."

The book *A Hundred White Daffodils* is a collection of the prose and poetry of the late poet Jane Kenyon. The section "Everything I Know About Writing Poetry" includes this advice: "Be a good steward of your gifts. Protect your time. Read good books. Be by yourself as often as you can. Walk."

I think it's important to observe the seasons of the year, to touch the earth, and to celebrate the feasts and festivals that have been bred into us for thousands of years. Sometimes that means celebrating alone. It's good to practice how to do it well. For Christmas, I buy myself little gifts throughout the year and tuck them away. "Is this for you?" one clerk asked me, "or do you want it gift-wrapped?"

"Yes," I said. "It's for me and I want it gift-wrapped."

A woman and I were comparing accounts of our Easter brunch. She'd had a peanut butter sandwich alone. I had made for myself a solitary feast, set the table with the best linen and flowers — and one plate. "I would never think of doing that just for myself," she said. Just me — that stingy phrase again. I'm following the advice from the poet Daniel Halpern: "Light the candles, pour the red wine into your glass. Before you eat, raise your glass in honor of yourself. The company is the best you'll ever know."

I grew up in an age when parents raised us with benevolent indifference. "Go outside and play," was the cry heard across the land. When they did focus attention on us, we were often rebellious or forgetful. Much of the time I didn't pay attention, but my mother taught me all her life. She taught me how to iron a white shirt, how to leave home and how to love life. Then she taught me how to die. And how to let things and people and animals I love die. That does not mean pain-free.

Elizabeth Cady Stanton's last speech was titled "The Solitude of Self." She was seventy-seven and had lived a rich life, married with a house full of children and campaigning across the country for women's rights. Maybe this speech was a culmination of everything she had learned and felt. One of the frequent arguments against giving women equal rights, she said, was men's desire to protect and support them. And sometimes, women's desire to be protected. But, she said, "when death sunders our nearest ties, alone we sit in the shadows of our affliction. Amid the greatest triumphs and darkest tragedies of life, we walk alone. We must make the voyage of life alone and for safety in an emergency, we must know something of the laws of navigation."

Being alone is hard. Doing nothing is harder. We are a society that worships busyness. We are as busy, to quote a chum, as rats on acid. We stay on the rim of life, says Richard Rohr in his book *Everything Belongs,* never reaching the quiet hub of the wheel or the heart of things. Instead, we adopt a false identify of What I have, What I do and What other people think of me.

That's what I wanted to say in my commentaries and in this book.

Degas could see Ingres' paintings even when he was blind. When I got glasses in the second grade, I was amazed to learn that the green part of trees was a bunch of separate leaves. I've always had poor vision. That is a metaphor for my whole life — trouble seeing things as they are. Sometimes that has had sour — and expensive —

results. Other times, I stumble along in blithe ignorance or suspended disbelief. Movies are a good example. I've been to movies with a cowboy who laughed all the way through a western, saying things like "That's not the same white horse he started on;" with an athlete who sneered at the actor's baseball throw; and with scornful musicians who pointed out that the music the actor was conducting on screen wasn't the music that was playing on the sound track. Try as I might, I couldn't see the same things they saw.

There's knowledge and there's criticism, and they may look alike, but they're not always the same enchilada. I worked at an advertising agency where we had an in-house axiom: *Where were you when the paper was blank?* Meaning, it's easier to criticize than to create.

Life is hard and it's harder if you're stupid. I don't know who said that, but I like it. It's hard and it's stressed and a lot of it is funny. Music comforts, and books. And what Angie Debo called "some creative work." Edith Wharton recommended "the discipline of the daily task." Energy, enthusiasm and humor help, like waxing the surfboard. As the reggae song says, "Lively up yourself."

When I was a little girl in Nowata, Oklahoma, I spent a lot of the summer hanging around Benjamin's funeral home. When the funeral home owners went away on a world trip, Mexico perhaps, or Colorado, they bought a toy for every child in town who had sent in his name. We never knew when, but one magical day the funeral home windows, which usually held plastic wreaths, would be transformed. Suddenly the plate glass windows were full of small toys and in front of every toy was a card such as, "Connie Jo, age 8." And in front of the window was a crowd of children looking for their name and toy. One year I got a tiny band of wooden frogs playing musical instruments.

Today we would cynically tag this as marketing or public relations. It never occurred to me then that it was advertising. For advertising, Benjamin's distributed paper fans with a colored picture of Jesus in the Garden of Gethsemane. We didn't think it was surreal that a funeral home was giving away toys. We didn't think it was a subtle campaign to brainwash us not to fear death. We just thought, Lucky us! Toys! Gifts came with the territory of being eight or nine. You had to come inside at dark and you had to get shots from a needle the size of a meat prong, but you got gifts for Christmas and for your birthday and from Benjamin's in the summer. That's life, jumbled together like my aunt's three-bean salad.

So, come on world, show me what you've got. It's not just me you're dealing with. This is Connie Cronley, Party of One.